AF492425

METAMORPHOSIS

Two Plays on Mahatma Gandhi

Shankar Prasad Tripathy

Translated By

Sanjeet Kumar Das

Copyright © Sankar Prasad Tripathy Translated by Sanjeet Kumar Das

All Rights Reserved.

This book has been self-published with all reasonable efforts taken to make the material error-free by the author. No part of this book shall be used, reproduced in any manner whatsoever without written permission from the author, except in the case of brief quotations embodied in critical articles and reviews.

The Author of this book is solely responsible and liable for its content including but not limited to the views, representations, descriptions, statements, information, opinions and references ["Content"]. The Content of this book shall not constitute or be construed or deemed to reflect the opinion or expression of the Publisher or Editor. Neither the Publisher nor Editor endorse or approve the Content of this book or guarantee the reliability, accuracy or completeness of the Content published herein and do not make any representations or warranties of any kind, express or implied, including but not limited to the implied warranties of merchantability, fitness for a particular purpose. The Publisher and Editor shall not be liable whatsoever for any errors, omissions, whether such errors or omissions result from negligence, accident, or any other cause or claims for loss or damages of any kind, including without limitation, indirect or consequential loss or damage arising out of use, inability to use, or about the reliability, accuracy or sufficiency of the information contained in this book.

Made with ❤ on the Notion Press Platform

www.notionpress.com

METAMORPHOSIS

CONTENTS

IN GANDHI'S ROLE

&

GANDHI IN ODISHA

Mahatma Gandhi visited Odisha eight times before the country's Independence. His first visit was on 23 March 1921. When he was travelling from Calcutta (Kolkata) to Madras (Chennai) on his last visit, the people of Odisha welcomed him at Balasore, Bhadrak, and Cuttack Railway Stations, and he delivered his last speech at the Berhampur (Brahmapur) Station on 19 January 1946. Later, on 15 August, India gained Independence. The play sheds light on the *Charkha* Movement, *Khadi* Movement, Voice against Untouchability, Quit Government Job Movement, Quit India Movement, Salt Satyagraha Movement and *Harijan Padayatra*. The play includes Gandhi's eight-time visit, his relationship with Odisha and the various accounts of the movements in Odisha during the struggle for India's Independence. On the eve of celebrating the Centenary Year of Mahatma Gandhi's visit to Odisha, this play *Gandhi in Odisha* was staged by the Department of Language, Literature and Culture, Government of Odisha, all over Odisha on 23 March 2023 and earned huge acclamation.

Gandhi's philosophy and lifestyle are confined to textbooks. Rarely are they reflected in real life. The hero of the play, coming to learn something in life, becomes a culprit in the eyes of politics. Some events in the criminal world force him to change and subsequently regulate his lifestyle. There is a need for finance/money for this. He is assured that he will receive cash if Gandhi's Statue is installed. So, being a Gandhi for a single day would help him ruin the government's money, but he fell in love with Gandhi's philosophy. Throughout his life, he has practised Gandhi's ideology in real life. But today's world has not allowed him to live as another Gandhi. He has suffered a lot. Thus, the protagonist succumbs to pressure in the political domain and the competitive market of the business world.

At last, he loses his way, being hoodwinked in all spheres of the society. He loses his job and wife subsequently. Nobody pays him any respect in the society. He has lost his dignity. Still, he dreams and has faith in the social system that the night's darkness will disappear and the sun will shine soon. This play, *In Gandhi's Role*, ushered a unique place in the hearts of Odia people when it was staged in more than a hundred places all over Odisha at a time.

SANKAR PRASAD TRIPATHY

TRANSLATOR'S VIEW

One of the leading playwrights of contemporary Odia Literature is Sankar Prasad Tripathy, who has extensively worked to highlight the unique ethnicity of the Odia race for the world to appreciate. In this 'work of art,' *Metamorphosis*, I have translated two of his Odia plays, *Gandhi Bhumikare* and *Gandhinka Odisha*, as *In Gandhi's Role* and *Gandhi in Odisha*, respectively. Both the plays are based on Mahatma Gandhi, 'Father of the Nation' and his philosophy.

Let's first understand that the title of the book is *Metamorphosis*. Metamorphosis is a complete dramatic change or transformation of a literary character or form. This transformation may sometimes happen at the individual or social levels. In the first play, *In Gandhi's Role*, the main protagonist, Ramdas, is initially introduced as a ruffian or hooligan with other company characters. Later, getting a chance to play the role of Gandhi in the celebration of *Gandhi Jayanti* (Birthday Celebration of Mahatma Gandhi, i.e., 02 October) organized with the installation of Gandhi's Statue at the *Golei Chowk*, he fell in love with the role and ideology or philosophy of Gandhi till he breathes his last. In the play, Ramdas is marked as practising Gandhism in real life. He gives up his earlier practices like selling cinema tickets in black, pickpocketing, collecting tips from the business people in the society and trying to live the life of a gentleman. His simplicity and innocence in social life are observed. But society still needs to approve of his present role. Wearing *khadi* clothes (*Dhoti* and Shawl), a pair of goggles, holding the *Gita* in one hand and a staff in the other, Ramdas walks on the street to help people. Nobody in the society accepts him. He has encountered people in different domains of life. To earn his livelihood, he wanders door to door and works there for a month, requesting them to pay him for his work. He identifies hypocrisy in their face and returns empty-handed. He is consecutively cheated by a politician and his team members, a businessman, and a film producer in the play.

In the end, he is ruined. People slam him, laugh at his lifestyle and enjoy his accuracy in the role. But they don't pay him what's due. At the end of the play, Ramdas loses his wife. He couldn't do his wife Chandramukhi's operation and was admitted to the hospital due to the shortage of money. Though he works in different organizations, he is not paid. He has not retaliated against the owners anywhere. His love is finally lost. When he sees the politician rapes his wife, he raises his voice against him. He promises to his wife that he will never be Ramdas again. His conscience hurts him not to be involved in any antisocial activity. Like Gandhi, he says, "The law will take its course."

As the story unfolds, Ramdas says that my father disapproved of my mother's love when I came into the world first. My mother asked his father for my identity, and he discarded it vehemently. She was forced to go to the city alone when I was a small kid. City people also didn't pay her any respect. The moment Ramdas came to realize this, he tried to understand her situation when he got the shocking news that her mother had had cancer for a long time and had died. People of the city treated her as a prostitute. Then, he becomes a hooligan as per the situational need. He was experiencing a financial setback.

Here, thug/rowdy Ramdas becomes Mahatma Gandhi. One who believes in violence gives up his profession and adopts Gandhi's attitude and behaviour, appears in Gandhi's get-up in real life and follows the path of nonviolence. His dress code and conduct are wholly metamorphosed. The story resembles the life of Saint Valmiki, who wrote the Great Indian Epic *The Ramayan*. His childhood name was Valmiki, a well-known bandit. The play also hints at the plights of people experiencing poverty. Ramdas loves to play Gandhi's role, but society does not allow him to live with prestige and dignity. He gets defeated everywhere in life. In Aristotelian terms, here is *peripeteia* (A sudden reversal of fate), a concept that is designed to bring complexity to the plot of any work of art.

In the second play, *Gandhi in Odisha*, the playwright gives a historical account of Gandhi's visit to Odisha and how his entry into the land triggers the people's psyche for social transformation. His honesty and simplicity created an aura in the surroundings. Due to the magnetic power of this charismatic aura, people from different corners of India gradually inclined to him and united to stand against the British Government. Gandhiji's first visit to Odisha was on 23 March 1921. When the people of Odisha suffered from natural calamities, he collected funds from the rest of the country and used them for the welfare of the people of Odisha. He suggested that Gopabandhu Das take an initiative where low-income people could work and earn their livelihood. He thought of people with low incomes most of the time. He advocated installing spinning wheels at each individual's house to develop the economic condition of the people. Freedom fighters like Gopabandhu Das, Nilakantha Das, Ramadevi, Gopabandhu Choudhury, Harekrushna Mahatab, and Harihar Das supported him strongly. People from different parts of Odisha willingly came forward to extend their cooperation to the much loved 'Bapu' to release the country from the autocratic ruler of the British Government. Their love and support are marked and widely discussed in historical events like the Salt Satyagraha Movement, Non-Cooperation Movement, Quit India Movement, *Harijan Padayatra*, Boycotting of foreign goods, and giving up government jobs by the youth. His magical spell has been well-perceived in the state well—his support for reorganizing the State of Odisha based on language before the British Government is unforgettable. Then Odisha state was formed on 01 April 1936. His last visit to Odisha was on 19 January 1946. He was thinking of the economic development of the country and the social upliftment of the Dalits (Harijan). For the betterment of the conditions of the Harijans, he has arranged several *padayatras* in Odisha. He didn't enter the temple, saying my people, especially the Harijans, were not allowed to enter. He raised his voice strongly against untouchability, casteism, and the evil social prejudices in India.

At last, he was the man to lead the country in marching on the path of 'Truth and Nonviolence'. He was an apostle of Truth and Nonviolence. He is respected worldwide for this approach in life. Under his clarion call, the whole country united and raised its voices against the lethal and tyrannical

British Government for Independence. He is an unforgettable hero of the land.

His character is focused in both the plays by the playwright. In the second play, the real Gandhi is revered in society, while in the second play, Ramdas, in Gandhi's role, is not accepted by the people in the society. Gandhi represents truth, nonviolence, simplicity, and honesty. Ramdas practices these attributes in his life. He is completely changed in real life. He is dramatically changed from a thug to Gandhi in real life. He is metamorphosed. The first play hints at the individual level metamorphosis, while the second Drama shows social Metamorphosis. One call of Gandhiji united India and subsequently brought Independence to the country and drove the foreign force, the British Government, away from the land. The second play talks of social Metamorphosis. The title chosen for the book is adequately justified.

While translating the Odia plays of the playwright into English, the rules and regulations of the target language, English, are paid due attention. Some lexical entries of the Odia language are retained as they are for their cultural uniqueness.

I want to thank the playwright Sankar Prasad Tripathy for having faith in me to translate two of his Odia plays into English here.

I want to thank the managing director and his crew

members of Notions Press for their kind consent and timely action in publishing the work of art on time.

SANJEET KUMAR DAS

In Gandhi's Role

A play does not aim at arresting the audience or the readers with its natural or unnatural spell or to induce excitement in them. So, the story is narrated indifferently. It's, for me, an unrealistic world, and the incidents are born out of natural or unnatural situations in society; it is the conglomeration of mixed feelings in dreams and reality. All the characters in the play wear uniforms so as not to create misconceptions. One character acts differently in different circumstances. The characters wearing a particular dress code indicate they are not the characters but the stage manager, interpreters, or annotators. By doing that, the play encompasses different dimensions. So, not paying attention to the natural flow of the actors, the audience and readers should be conscious of the particular role of the character in a specific scene. When acting from one role to the other, the characters can be adequately justified if the actors adopt changes in their dialogue delivery and gestures. No props, montage, or setting will be used in the play. The play has been scripted in street play or open theatre format. So, when staging, the directors will pay due attention to the play.

A black screen is at the back of the stage. A block is in the middle. There is clamour heard. It's one of the squares of the city. Three young men stand holding ticket books in their hands. They sell tickets to the audience through mime. They are the workers of the Yuvak Sangh. They collect fees for installing the Gandhi statue in *Gandhi Jayanti* (Birth Anniversary of Mahatma Gandhi). They are Actor I, Actor II and Actor III.

DRAMATIS PERSONAE

Actor I   : A Hooligan initially, later Assistant to the
Minister

Actor II   : A Hooligan initially, later Assistant to the
Minister

Actor III   : A Hooligan initially, later the role of
Ramdas, and the role of Gandhi

Rabi   : Poet intially, later Business Man

Soma   : Teacher, Poet, Film Producer

Mangala   : Teacher, Poet, Assistant to the Minister

Minister

Inspector

Chandramukhi/

Chandra   : A female Hooligan married to Ramdas

[Most of the characters do multiple roles in this play.]

Actor I	: Good Morning, Sir!
Actor II	: Good Morning!
Actor III	: Sir, Good Morning!
Actor I	: We have come from *Golei Chowk*.
Actor II	: We will celebrate *Gandhi Jayanti*.
Actor-III square.	: We will install the Gandhi Statue on the

Actor I : We don't ask for fees for any cinema or theatre. On the eve of the next *Gandhi Jayanti* (02 October), one statue of Mahatma Gandhi will be installed on *Golei Chowk*. Please buy a ticket. (One person buys a ticket.)

Actor II : Twenty One rupees only? Sorry, Sir. You make unnecessary expenditures. Please donate something for Gandhiji. Permanent work will be for the people. It will only be suitable if you give Rs. 100/- rupees.

Actor III : We came here thrice and returned. Two more days left for the Gandhi Jayanti; how can we organize such a big event without your help? Or else pay at least fifty-one rupees.

Actor I : We are inviting the minister. He will inaugurate the function.

Actor II   : There will be a meeting. We must arrange flower bouquets, snacks and the people for the meeting. We will spend Rs. 10,000/- to build a Gandhi statue. Where will we get money?

[The actors realized. The people who bought tickets are no longer there. There are few tickets left. All of them are exhausted and sit on a block.]

Actor II   : It was going on for a month. What have you arranged?

Actor I   : The Minister has consented. Flower garlands and snack packets are also ordered. We only have to think of the Gandhi Statue.

Actor II   : Only two more days have yet to be finalized. You have taken responsibility for that.

Actor I   : Whatever the situation, we will finalize this today. Otherwise, nobody will build the statue in less time. (While they converse with each other, Actor-III sells tickets outside. He comes to sit on the block after selling all the tickets.)

Actor III   : I have sold all the tickets.

Actor I   : How much did you collect?

Actor III   : By yesterday, the collection amount was ten thousand. Today, I have sold tickets for three books. So the total collection will be twelve thousand plus.

Actor II   : Wandering from door to door for one month, it is only twelve thousand. Yes, have you ever collected more than this before? (Looking at Actor I) to you?

Actor I   : No-

Actor II   : (Looking at Actor III) To you?

Actor III   : No-

[All actors on the stage come to the audience's front. They are introducing themselves.]

Actor II   : I am the cinema ticket blacker, Sunny. I don't get more than eight hundred rupees selling tickets in black.

Actor I   : I am the pick picket, Vicky. I get something more than that. There is no certainty in the collection, but it is risky.

Actor III   : I am Rama Das, the hooligan of the *Golei Chowk*. My job is hooliganism. Sometimes, we have a good collection; sometimes, we are empty-handed. But we, three, are the workers of *Golei Chowk Yuvak Sangh*. We collect fees in the name of Gandhi.

Actor III	: Whatever the case may be, our income is good.
Actor I	: Leave that. What about the Gandhi Statue?
Actor II	: (Looking at Actor III) Have you made any enquiries?
Actor III	: Building a six-foot statue of Plaster of Parish will cost eight thousand rupees.
Actor I	: How much?
Actor III	: Eight thousand only. That too plaster of parish.
Actor II	: Eight thousand. What will be with us if we spend eight thousand out of twelve thousand? We will get only four thousand working for the entire month. The proposal is rejected. Where can we do cheaper than that amount?
Actor II	: It will cost only six thousand if we build it in cement.
Actor I	: Can you repeat?
Actor II	: Six thousand? Forget that. We can't buy the statue for that amount. Think of another way to build the same with less than six thousand.

Actor III   : Then the earthen statue will be cheaper. That will cost around three thousand rupees. But, it is not possible within two days.

Actor I   : If not in two days, we will postpone the inaugural function of the statue for some more days. Is the amount OK for all?

Actor III   : Then it can't be possible. This is final.

Actor II   : No, this is not final. What do you think? We request the people, like anything, to get a sum of a hundred rupees, "Sir, we have come from *Golei Chowk Yuvak Sangh* to install a Gandhi Statue. Please pay us the fees." You are here to pay three thousand rupees without giving any second thought.

Actor III   : Well, but one photo of Gandhiji to install there. Only three hundred rupees have to be spent.

Actor II   : Yes, do that.

Actor I   : Shut up. Will the people accept if you install the photo instead of the statue?

Actor II   : You are right. We would have stolen if the city had been with a Gandhi Statue anywhere. That's not possible.

Actor I   : Can we get the Gandhi Statue free of cost anywhere?

[All pray Gandhiji.]

Actor-II	: Hey Gandhi! Where will we get you freely? We have collected twelve thousand rupees. That could have been ours.

[An idea comes to the mind of Actor III.]

Actor III	: An idea-
Actor II & III	: (In unison) What's the idea?
Actor III	: The idea is-
Actor I	: What's then?
Actor III	: How long should Gandhi's statue be here? When will we return the statue if we get it by chance?
Actor I	: At least one hour until the meeting is over.
Actor III	: Then it's possible free of cost.
Actor II	: Free of cost! We will have this twelve thousand. Where will we get it?
Actor III	: (To Actor I) Can you call a barber?
Actor I	: Barber- should he be with a razor?
Actor III	: Yes or no?
Actor I	: Yes, One barber is our neighbour. I can call him.
Actor III	: (To Actor II) Your father must have *dhoti*. You will also bring goggles/spectacles.

Actor II   : Yes, I can. What will you do with all these?

Actor III   : Hold on. I will arrange a staff and the *Gita*.

Actor I   : Is there any need?

Actor   III   :   Gandhi!

Actor I & II   : Gandhi?

Actor III   : Yes, I will be Gandhi. The barber will come to shave my head. I will wear a *dhoti*, hold a staff and stand up. [Both of them laugh.]

Actor I & II : You (They laugh again.)

Actor III   : Why are you laughing?

[They laugh loudly.]

Actor III   : Shut up! I am asking why you are laughing.

Actor I   : Nay, you are rightly looking like Gandhi.

Actor II   : Your physique, face, and attributes resemble Gandhi completely. Who is better than you here to become Gandhi?

Actor I   : My brother! If you want us to be beaten by the people, I request you not to become Gandhi publicly.

Actor III   : I ask you why I can't be.

Actor I	: Have you ever seen Gandhiji?
Actor III	: No-
Actor II	: Have you ever read about Gandhiji?
Actor III	: I am a class-IV fail. You are asking me about qualifications.
Actor I	: You are engaged in hooliganism and murdering people. You say you will be Gandhi. We will stay safe if you don't become Gandhi.
Actor III	: I swear I will be Gandhi. Are those who act Ramachandra's role in the Opera gentlemen? Are they saints?
Actor I	: No-
Actor III	: Do they look like Ramachandra?
Actor II	: No-
Actor III	: If the thief Ramia becomes Ramachandra, why can't the hooligan Ramadas be Gandhi?
Actor I	: Yes, you can.
Actor III	: So, I can act in Gandhi's role.
Actor II	: Then, the work is done.
Actor III	: I have to stand for one hour. Once the meeting is over, I will go.
Actor II	: Well, he has come up with a good idea.

Actor I   : Let's go for arranging all the props.

[All leave the stage. The stage is lit off. After the light, Actor III (Ramadas) is seen waiting for someone on a road in the city. Two teachers are coming from the school on that road. They are Soma and Mangal. Actor III says 'pranam' to them.]

Actor III   : Good morning, Sir! Thanks God! I have seen you here. Otherwise, I would have gone to you. I have an urgent work with you.

Soma   : Do you have a work with me? You are not joking, Ramadas! I am an ordinary teacher in the school. I have been staying here for so many days. Have you ever come to me for any work?

Actor III   : But today, I need you earnestly.

Soma   : Then you say what you need me for.

Actor III   : Sir, you are teaching the students. You must know Gandhi.

Soma   : Gandhi-I can't understand you.

Actor III   : Gandhi-whose photos are installed on the office walls - about whom the politicians always speak in *Gandhi Jayanti*. I am talking about Gandhi.

Mangal   : Oh! Are you talking about Mahatma Gandhi?

Actor III   : Yes, that Gandhi-

Soma   : Do you have any work to do with him?

Actor III: Do you have any knowledge about him? How does he look? What does he wear? How does he generally stand up?

Soma   : Yes- I know something about him.

Actor III: Can you tell me what I need to act like Gandhi?

Soma   : To be Gandhi is more challenging. For that, you need sacrifice, sincerity, and patriotism.

Actor III   : Leave that. I am talking about those who acted in Gandhi's role.

Soma   : Oh, are you talking about that role? Who will act in Gandhi's role?

Actor III   : I will!

Mangala   : You? (Surprisingly)

Actor III   : We couldn't get Gandhi's statue. So, I will stand up in Gandhi's role for an hour. Sir, please don't say this to anybody. It will be critical if you tell others.

Soma   : Ramadas! Will you be Gandhi? I can't believe this.

Actor III   : I will be Gandhi for an hour. We will save twelve thousand rupees that we have collected from selling the tickets. That will be ours.

Soma   : Ramdas! If you become Gandhi for an hour, you will earn Rs 12,000/-. But if you become Gandhi throughout your life, what you will gain can't be compared.

Actor III   : Leave that. Gandhi was a great man where Gandhi is, where I am. What clothes will I need to do Gandhi's role?

Soma   : You need simple clothes: A coarse dhoti, a coarse shawl, a pair of round glasses and a staff. A pendulum with a chain is to be hung at the waist.

Actor III   : Well, I will collect all those. Sir, how does Gandhi stand up?

Soma   : You have to learn that. (To Mangala) You will train him.

Mangal   : I-

Soma   : Yes.

Actor III   : (To Mangala) Can you be available at home in the evening? I will call you. He will be Gandhi in one day- (Soma is laughing.) You are laughing.

Soma   : These are Gandhi's outer get-up. But there is a need for internal changes.

Actor III   : What do you mean?

Soma   : How was Gandhi walking? He was weaving threads in a spinning wheel. He was reading the *Bhagavad Gita* every day.

Actor III   : How will you do all this?

Soma   : If you are interested, Sir will train you everything. Everything is possible with your endeavour and perseverance. One day, you will see that you are no longer Ramadas but Mohandas.

Actor III   : Now I am in trouble. I would not have taken this task if I had known this much difficulty for only twelve thousand rupees.

Soma   : Why do you think this is a problem? It's not difficult at all. Everything will be set right gradually.

Actor III   : How can it be done in one night? We will celebrate *Gandhi Jayanti* tomorrow.

Soma   : Your foundation will be laid. You can get at least one chapter of the *Gita* by heart. Then you will see-

Actor III   : No need to continue that role after that. I will have no work after the meeting is over tomorrow. Then, who asks Gandhi? OK, I'll leave now. I have so many works. Sir, (To Mangala) I will meet you in the evening.

Mangala : You have troubled me, Sir. I can't assure you that Ramadas will learn. Wearing a piece of dhoti as Gandhi, he would stand for an hour. What was the need to train him in the Bhagavat or Gita?

Soma : Of the number of scriptural texts written in the world for the welfare of society, the *Gita* is the best. The knowledge, philosophy and means of character building are well enunciated in this text. The thread becomes a garland with the touch of flowers, so the wicked ones get changed into virtuous characters by reading the Bhagavad Gita.

Mangala : That's not possible for a goon like Ramadas.

Soma : Mangala, the pirate Ratnakar, also becomes the great poet, Valmiki, chanting the name of Lord Rama. What was there in that name that changed Ratnakar's character? The influence of each word, from a scientific angle, affects our body. The word 'Rama' has influenced Ratnakar so well that the poetic lines stream or flow from his heart. The influence of the Gita may change Ramadas.

Mangala : How will you benefit from this?

Soma   : Today, the entire world is oppressed by the Ramadases. What's the way to avoid them? There is a need for one Gandhi. Otherwise, there will be bloodshed everywhere, and the world will be chaotic and violent.

Mangala   : Why can't I accept this thought now?

Soma   : You have been teaching throughout your life. You have taught so many students. You have asked them about their goals in life. Some have told you to be a doctor or Engineer; some might have told you to join Indian Administrative Services; some might have shown interest in business tycoons, etc. Have you ever marked anyone to say that I will be Gandhi in life?

Mangala   : Why will one say so?

Soma   : But today, one hooligan says to be Gandhi-

Mangala   : For an hour only-

Soma   : A significant change may happen in a minute. One hour is enough. You are the teacher; this is the time for a great test. If you are successful, you will accomplish the significance of your teaching.

Mangala   : It is like "a futile effort". You will think of what comes to your mind and drag us to the danger. Well, I have assured him to help in the evening. Let's go.

[Soma smiles silently. The stage light is off. It's evening. Mangala gets irritated while training Ramadas and is ready to leave his home. The Gita is in one of Ramadas's hands. He is pulling Mangala not to go. Then there is the stage light.]

Actor III : Please listen to me. I have to read this book tonight.

Mangala : Impossible task! It would help if you remembered everything. How can I help you remember this text? Nobody can remember the *Gita* in one night- impossible.

Actor III : Then what sort of teacher are you?

Mangala : That's why we need time. How can it be done when you say? These are Sanskrit verses.

Actor III : How did your head, Sir, say?

Mangala : He is a mad person. What will you get from his words? You can't utter Sanskrit words correctly; how will you remember the book? You can go now. have your food and then sleep at night. This is not your work.

Actor III : (Showing a knife) O master! I say you submissive to teach me; otherwise, I will throw your legs severing from your body.

Mangala : How can I forcibly teach you?

Actor III   : How can you deny it? Everything is possible through money. You have come to teach me free of cost. Teach me-

Mangala   : I am in trouble now. Ok, you read: "*akhaṇḍa maṇḍalākāraṁ vyāptajena carācaraṁ*"

Actor III   : So much at a time? Teach me word by word. Am I a college student?

Mangala   : *a-kha-ṇḍa*

Actor III   : *a...a...kh...a...ṇḍ...a*

Mangala   : It's not '*ḍa*', but '*ṇḍa*'- *akhaṇḍa*

Actor III   : It's not '*ḍa*', but '*ṇḍa*'- *akhaṇḍa*

Mangala   : Oh! It's *ṇ-ḍ-ṇḍ*. The word is *akhaṇḍa*.

Actor III   : '*ṇḍa*' [Mangala teaches, and Actor III learns; he gets annoyed as Actor III cannot pronounce the sounds correctly. He can't pronounce the word '*akhaṇḍa*' till the end.]

Mangala   : Reading is difficult for you. Instead, you spend time in hooliganism.

Actor III   : You are a teacher. You know everything.

Mangala   : Yes.

Actor III   : (Showing many poses of Karate to Mangala) Can you do?

Mangala   : Can I?

Actor III   : Yes [Mangala tries, but all are wrong.]

Mangala   : *U-ha-hi...ho-*

Actor III   : Shut up. Practise the poses silently.

[While Mangala is practising, Actor III is reading the *Gita*.]

Actor III   : *"akhaṇḍa mandalākāram vyāptajena carācaram"*-

[At this critical moment, the lover of Actor III, Ms Chandramukhi, reaches there. She wears jeans and a T-shirt. She has a masculine style and unnatural behaviour. Miss Chandramukhi is a fantasy in this grim reality. She is the one who can lead from the real world to an unnatural imaginative world. She seems to be a lady pirate in the cinema. She comes seriously, smokes a cigar and stares at Actor III in surprise.]

Chandramukhi: Hi...Handsome!

[Actor III does not show any reaction to her expression. But Mangala stops practising karate and looks at Chandralukhi.]

Mangala   : Hello-

[Having seen Mangala and his style, Chandramukhi invites him with pretention.]

Chandramukhi: Come - "Who are you to obstruct here?"

Mangala   : Hello [Chandramukhi slaps Mangala while he comes to her.]

Chandramukhi: Run- you scoundrel-

Mangala   : Ouch (Mangala runs from the place. Chandramukhi comes to Actor III and teases him for his sincerity in reading.)

Chandramukhi: Hi-

Actor III   : (I am reading.) *"akhaṇḍa maṇḍalākāram"*

Chandra   : My darling, you are reading. What is this going on?

Actor III   : *Gita-*

Chandra   : *Gita-* (She is laughing.) Reading of Gita in Mafia Don Miss Chandramukhi's area? How come?

Actor III   : You leave now, or you will see what I can do.

Chandra   : What did you say?

Actor III   : Don't disturb me. You can leave now.

Chandra   : You rascal- so much courage. You don't know me. When a child cries at the deadly hour of the night, the mother helps her child sleep in the bed, saying Miss Chandramukhi is coming. The dog can also leave the place submissively. But you disrespect me now.

Actor III : *"akhaṇḍa maṇḍalākāraṁ vyāptajena carācaraṁ"*

Chandra : Stop Sanskrit couplets. Are you reading lessons before Chandramukhi?

Actor III : Why are you shouting here?

Chandra : 'Revenge'. 'Revenge of your faithlessness' Can you remember the day when we first met each other? You stared at me and ran after me for ten minutes. At last, you said, "I love you, Chandramukhi."

Actor III : Please shut up!

Chandra : Nobody returns empty-handed from Miss Chandramukhi's Hall of Residence. I said, "I am pleased at your love. Amen! You love me- I love you too. But today?"

Actor III : What today?

Chandra : How are you reading Gita today?Nay-

Actor III : Why have you come here?

Chandra : 'For love' Ramadas, you return me your love! You return me your love!!

Actor III : It is dried up. It's no more in my heart.

Chandra : Dried up? Ears, have you heard Ramdas rightly? He has no love for me. How come it gets dried up?

Actor III : Chandramukhi, I am very sorry. I apologize for you leaving me for this night only. I have many works.

Chandra : What sort of work?

Actor III : I will read *Gita.* I will practise 'the manner of walking'. I will be Gandhi tomorrow in the meeting.

Gandhi : Gandhi, you? You are a hooligan and wicked fellow. You will be nowhere.

Actor III : I don't fear to die. I am afraid of living like this. I have lived like a dog, getting insults and contempt from others. I have earned money like an animal. Today, I got a chance to take on the role of a great person. I will be Gandhi for an hour only. I will hide my wicked nature under the mask of Gandhi Statue for an hour. People will forget Ramdas. They will surrender and pay respect at my feet, thinking of me as Gandhi. My sins, environment, and appearance will only be hidden or lost for that time. I have never been good to others or received any respect from them. What can be better than that moment for a hooligan like Ramdas? Let a hooligan take advantage of the opportunity to act pretentiously in the great man's role for an hour.

Chandra : Hey- you are talking like an educated person. Are you mad? What has happened to you? Can a hooligan be a great man? You know Ramdas, once a jackal, became a king of the forest being coloured in blue. All the creatures obeyed him. The day its nature was revealed, none of them pardoned the jackal. Ramdas, you have been mad.

Actor-III : Yes, yes- I am mad now. I need to be the king coloured in blue. He utters, *"akhaṇḍa maṇḍalākāraṁ vyāptajena carācaraṁ"*

Chandra : Chandramukhi, you listen to me. Your lover is going to die. He will be *Brahmarakshas*. Ramdas, you will die. After your death, you will appear as a drumstick tree in my homestead. I love to eat the drumstick leaves recipe. Every day, I will eat the recipe, especially *sāg* from that tree, and I will remember you. Go to hell, and be a drumstick tree. [Chandramukhi leaves the place. Actor III smiles silently and rereads *Gita.*]

Actor III : *"akhaṇḍa maṇḍalākāraṁ vyāptajena carācaraṁ,*

    tatpadaṁ darśitam jena tasmai śri gurave namah."

[The stage is lit off. A patriotic song is played inside. It's the minister's residence. It is 10 a.m. Actor-I calls.]

Actor I : Is the Honorable Minister at home?

[The undergarments of a woman are thrown towards the Actor-I. He is worried.]

Actor I : (Loudly) Is the minister at home? [An empty wine bottle comes rolling down to him.]

Actor I : Oh my God! Is the Honorable Minister at home?

[The Minister has come intoxicated. A feeding bottle is at his face. He always drinks wine from that. For the ordinary people, that's a milk bottle.]

Minister : Whom are you searching for?

Actor I : Honourable Minister!

Minister : Nobody is here in that name.

Actor I : You are the minister.

Minister : Who said? I am a minister, but not *Mantri*.

Actor I : That's the same, Sir.

Minister : OK, all right. Then I am here. What's your need?

Actor I   : Sir, I am from *Golei Chowk Yuvak Sangh*. You are becoming our guest today.

Minister   : You will be the 'guest'. What's that?

Actor I   : We will invite you to the meeting where you will deliver your speech.

Minister   : What's unique about the day?

Actor I   : *Gandhi Jayanti-*

Minister   : Which Gandhi?

Actor I   : Mahatma Gandhi-

Minister   : Oh, so many Gandhis are here. It's tough to remember their *Jayanti* (Birth Anniversary). How come *Gandhi Jayanti* comes so early? As our village teacher says, it is on 30 January.

Actor I   : No, Sir. Today is mentioned in the calendar.

Minister   : What is right? Whether the Calendar or the village teacher's word?

Actor I   : The calendar is correct because the government has published it.

Minister   : Yes, you are right. I will attend the meeting. Hear me. Is the audience there in the meeting?

Actor I   : Sir, more than one thousand-

Minister   : Where did you bring them?

Actor I   : We have brought some of them from the village by trucks, while the rest are from nearby places.

Minister   : All right. I will go. My dress is under pressure. Once it is over, I will reach there.

Actor I   : Sir, Fees-

Minister   : For what?

Actor I   : We don't invite anybody as a guest without fees. Your guest fees-

Minister   : (Smiling) No guest without fees?

Actor I   : No, Sir-

Minister   : OK, Come to me (Actor–I comes to him.)

Minister   : Sit down here.

Actor I   : Will I sit down?

Minister   : Yes- Won't you take 'fees'?

Actor I   : Yes, Sir (He sits down.)

Minister   : Open your mouth-

Actor I   : What to do, Sir? Why will I open my mouth?

Minister   : I will give you 'fees'. Don't worry.

Actor I   : Yes, I opened my mouth. [When he opens his mouth, the minister pours a drop of wine from the feeding bottle.]

Minister   : Now you can go-

Actor I   : This is wine. Where's the 'fee'?

Minister   : Shut up. This is the scented milk.

Actor I   : OK. Please give me the 'fee'.

Minister   : You have drunk. What's fee?

Actor I   : we won't get back the money we spent on the meeting. So I will get the fees from you before I leave.

Minister   : He won't allow me to leave. OK, you can go now. You will take this after the meeting is over.

Actor-I   : Sir, I am leaving now. Good day!

[Actor-I leaves. The stage is lit off while the minister enters inside, strolling. After the light comes, a square of the city is seen. Gandhi Statue will be installed, and a meeting will be held. Actor I and Actor II are engaged in the arrangement and decoration of the stage. Actor III has come, covering his body with a shawl. Having seen him, Actor-I gets terrified.]

Actor I   : Gho…st

Actor II   : Ghost? Where? Where is the ghost?

Actor I   : Here is the ghost. (Showing the Actor-III)

Actor II   : A ghost in the daytime. Thrash him. (He has gone to beat him.)

Actor III   : Hold on. What are you doing?

Actor I   : Ramdas- You are here. We are unable to recognize you.

Actor III   : (Taking off the shawl from his body) Can you see whether I look like Gandhi? [Actor-III has already taken the makeup.]

Actor II   : Absolutely Gandhi!

Actor I   : How have you taken the makeup?

Actor II   : Hold on. Hey Ramdas, have you practised Gandhi's Role well?

Actor III   : Yes. Can you hear? (He chants.)

> "akhaṇḍa maṇḍalākāraṁ vyāptajena carācaraṁ,
>
> tatpadaṁ darśitam jena tasmai śri gurave namah."

Actor I   : What's this?

Actor III   : *Gita-*

Actor II   : Why is Gita needed?

Actor III   : Gandhi was reading the *Gita*. I will be standing as Gandhi. If anyone asks, I will chant the Sanskrit *sloka* (verses).

Actor I   : Awesome!

Actor III   : Do you want to see how Gandhiji was walking? You see (Actor-III walks like Gandhiji. He stands like Gandhiji.)

Actor I   : Hello, my dear; when did you learn all this?

Actor III   : Inviting the master, I have learnt throughout the night.

Actor I   : Then, it will be fantastic. You are the 'Living Gandhi'.

Actor Ii   : Shut up! Everything is smashed. People will pelt the rotten eggs, tomatoes, and worn-out slippers at us.

Actor I   : Why will they throw...?

Actor II   : Won't they? What this stupid Ramdas has shown before us is performed before the Minister. Can you think of the conditions we will undergo then and there?

Actor III   : Why will it be so?

Actor II   : Will you read the *Gita* before the Minister?

Actor III   : Yes, I will. Gandhi was reading *the Gita.*

Actor II   : Will you walk there?

Actor III   : I ask you why I can't do all this.

Actor II   : If you buy Gandhi's Statue, you will spend a lot. For that, you will stand still like a Gandhi Statue. Tell me, "Does a statue walk? Does it read *Gita*?"

Actor III   : You are right. The rascal master has told me lies throughout the night. Well, if anybody asks me-

Actor II   : You won't open your mouth. You will stand like a statue. Remember this.

Actor III   : Alright. Now, draw a curtain before my head.

Actor I   : Listen to me, you won't move at the time of inauguration. You won't shut your eyelid. You will be stiff.

Actor III   : OK. [Actor-III stands. Mosquitoes bite his legs. He kills them.] Oh, mosquitoes are here biting my legs. You will finish the meeting soon. I may tremble during the meeting.

[A taxi's horn is heard outside.]

Actor I   : Honorable Minister has reached. Actor-III is ready and others draw a curtain before his face. Brothers! (Looking at the audience roaming here and there) Don't stroll. Minister has come now. Please sit before the stage, maintaining silence. Chocolates will be distributed at the end of the meeting. [The Minister comes.]

Actor II   : Please come, Sir. Come to the stage. We have to set everything right. Sir, show your neck, please. We couldn't find the girls. Considering me as a girl, I garland you. Please show me your neck.

[Minister shows his neck, and Actor-II garlands him.]

Actor I   : Give a big round of applause. [There is clapping in the audience.]

Actor II   : Sir, please stand here for a while. Now we will sing 'Ramdhun'. We couldn't find the singers. We will sing 'Ramdhun' thinking of us as the singers. [They're singing.]

Both   : *"raghupati rāgham rājārām, patitapāban sitārām,*

īśwar āllah tere nām, sabko sanmati de bhagbān."

Actor I   : Now the meeting starts. As the president of the meeting, the Minister will preside over the session. (Clapping) I now request the honourable Minister to inaugurate or unveil the Statue. [Minister comes to the Gandhi Statue. Actor II gives a pair of scissors to the Minister. Minister cuts the ribbon. Actor-III stands as the Gandhi Statue.]

Minister : This is a lovely statue. (Minister touches the Statue.)

Actor I : Don't touch, Sir.

Minister : It's very soft.

Actor I : It is made of clay but needs to be dried up. It was painted a few minutes ago. If you touch it, its colour may fade away.

Minister : The Statue is very soft.

Actor II : (Showing the feet of Actor-III) Sir, bow down your head before the Gandhi Statue out of respect.

Minister : (Minister pays respect to Gandhi.) O my Lord! Remove my sorrows. (Then a mosquito bites the leg of Actor-III and his body trembles. The inebriated Minister stared at him, and, considering the Statue as an animal, he tried to get hold of him. Actor-III helps his leg move away from his clutch.)

Minister : Oh, why does it tremble?

Actor I : That's nothing. It seems to you that you have drunk a lot. [He says to Actor-II with a grave tone.] Stand upright.

Actor III   : How will I do? Mosquitoes bite. Oh-
               (Suddenly, the legs shake.)

Minister   : Hey, I am not intoxicated. You are
               intoxicated. This is an animal. I am sure this
               is a cobra. You see how he will listen to my
               padmatola mantras. [Minister sings.] *"ie
               vaṁśara gharaṇī, padmāvati rāṇī, kalāṇi
               dhanwantarī ośā ki govinda hari."* [Actor-II
               stops him with palms on his mouth.]

Actor II   : Sir, this is the stage. Do you think of it as
               the slum of Indian gypsies? Why do you
               lower your caste?

Minister   : Please shut up. I am telling you, this is a
               cobra. [When the Minister tries to catch hold
               of Actor-III, out of anger, he beats the
               Minister's head with the staff.]

Minister   : Ouch! Who beat me?

Actor I   : Nobody has beaten you. It's the stage for a
               meeting. Anybody can assault you. Sir, you
               come to the front to deliver your speech.

Actor II   : Sir, you will take less time for your speech.

Minister   : All right. (Minister delivers speech holding
               the microphone.) Ladies and gentlemen! It is
               a proud moment for all of us. The most
               successful story is that the country's youth,
               following Gandhi's ideology, installed
               Gandhiji's Statue at the square. Human

values are established in the country. Gandhi brought our country's independence through the weapons of truth and non-violence. But, the last Government of State Assembly didn't announce *Gandhi Jayanti* as the holiday. We have declared. From this, you can mark our respect for Gandhi.

Actor III : (In suppresses voice) Try to conclude the meeting soon. The mosquitoes bite me.

Actor I : Sir, please conclude your speech. The mosquitoes bite our legs.

Minister : I know the mosquitoes bite your legs. Still, then, you are sitting with patience. Our Government has planned a scheme to get rid of mosquitoes. Every block has an arrangement of selling bleaching powder and phenyl.

[Not seeing any hint of the Minister's speech ends, Actor-II says to Actor-I.]

Actor II : The Minister's speech will continue long. Cut off the microphone wire.

Actor I : OK [Actor-I cuts off the wire. But the Minister continues his speech.]

Minister : The mosquitoes won't be seen in this city. Gandhi brought independence to our country through non-violence; we will control the mosquitoes through non-violence. (The audience shouts that they can't hear anything.) Hello…hello…

Actor I   : Please come. Here is the power cut.

Minister   : A considerable gathering is here. I could have spoken more. Here is the power cut. The people working in the Department of Electricity and the State Government don't care about me. Alright, I will punish them.

Actor I   : Sir, please come.

Minister   : Well, I will wait here for half an hour. You set right the electricity. I will speak again.

Actor II   : The people will shout, Sir. You have a programme outside. Please come.

Minister   : Let's move [Actor-II accompanies Minister.]

Actor I   : (To the audience) Brothers and sisters! The meeting is over now. You all can return. (To Actor-III) Gandhibaba! After the people leave the place, you will go away surreptitiously.

[Actor-II leaves the stage after clearing everything. Actor-III relaxes seeing the lonely stage. While he attempts to move away, Rabi, Soma and Mangala reach there. In this scene, these three poets are inebriated (addicted to smoking ganja). Having seen them, Actor-III forcefully stands up again.]

Rabi   : It is an excellent place. After the Gandhi statue was installed, it became a place for entertainment.

Soma   : From today onwards, we will sit here instead of resting on the cabin side.

Rabi   : This place is suitable for research. Loneliness is everywhere. The sweet smell of the drains nearby and excrement in the surroundings come here. The mosquitoes buzz here. Waste papers, dust and debris litter here and there, like the broken clouds in the sky. Amidst them stands the Father of the Nation, Mahatma Gandhi.

Soma   : At this time Kabi Sambrat Khoka Mohanty sings, "bagichāra nāã tinikoṇia, ethi rāti bhiḍa dina śun śāniā."

Mangala   : Stop it. Now, I am acquiring special knowledge here. I need intoxicating substances. There is no research we can think of without intoxicants.

Rabi   : I also think in the same line. We should smoke a slight ganja.

Soma   : Rabi, do you have some money?

Rabi   : I have nothing in my pocket. I bought lipstick for my wife with what I had.

Soma   : Mangala, are you with anything?

Mangala   : No, I am now penurious. Giving three hundred rupees to a fair complexioned lady for her dress and twenty-five rupees for her bangles, I am utterly ruined. It is, of course, for love.

Soma   : It would have been better if we had had some alcoholic liquor. My mouth gets dried up.

Mangala   : I can't see anything. I am searching for money.

Rabi   : The day is spent in vain. [He looks at the newly bought *Gita* near the Gandhi statue.] Hey- Mangala! Can you see anything?

Mangala   : What?

Rabi   : *Gita*. It is at Gandhiji's side. If we sell this, we will get ten rupees. This will be enough for our ganja.

Soma   : Oh! Gandhi wears new goggles. You can see. If we sell that, we can get an additional ten rupees.

Mangala   : Rabi, take off these two.

[Rabi goes to take off the goggles from his eyes and *Gita* from his hands.]

Rabi   : Brother, I don't have any *lungi*. Gandhi wears a new *dhoti*. I am taking this.

[Actor-III is worried.]

Soma   : Hold on- You will take this at late night. Don't touch now.

Mangala   : Rabi, you take these two now. Selling them in the square, you will bring some ganja. We are waiting for you here.

Rabi   : Alright. [Rabi leaves the place to sell goggles and *Gita* in the market.]

Mangala   : By Gandhi's grace, we have got something for our expenditures on ganja.

Soma   : I think of something else.

Mangala   : What?

Soma   : When there is a quarrel between the hamlets, if we step out with the staff, the police seize our staff. We don't need them from today onwards. Gandhi is with a good staff. We will take this staff from here when there is a dispute. Once it is over, we will put the same again in his hands. The police won't doubt us.

Mangala   : Yes, you are right. Good idea!

[Rabi has come with ganja.]

Soma   : Did you bring ganja?

Rabi   : Yes. While walking on the road, I saw a
person and sold him.

Mangala   : Well, load ganja in the small smoke pipe.

[Rabi and Mangala are preparing ganja.]

Rabi   : I have an idea, Brother.

Soma   : You have another idea.

Rabi   : The Government has declared that a
Gandhi Statue will be installed at the square
on the sea beach. If we removed Gandhi
from this place and sold it to the
Government, we would get five thousand
rupees.

Mangala   : Five thousand?

Soma   : But, whom shall we sell? Can't he know
that it is a stolen statue?

Rabi   : How can he know? We will change the
colour.

Soma   : Then it's OK. How will we take it?

Mangala   : Is it a question? Darkness spreads
everywhere. Nobody comes to this side at
night. We will shoulder the Statue.

Rabi   : Then, why are you sitting? Let's stop taking ganja. After transferring Gandhi and hiding somewhere, we will enjoy ganja. Catch hold of it now.

[Rabi, Soma, and Mangala have come to Actor-III. He is afraid of them first. When they try to hold him, his body trembles.]

Mangala   : Hey, how come the Gandhi's Statue is so soft?

Rabi   : It is made of cement and has not dried thoroughly. So, taking this, we must first bake the Statue in the fire. Then, if we colour its body, it won't be ruined.

Soma   : Hold it tightly. Let's say, "*Jay Gandhi Baba Ki*"

[While Rabi, Soma and Mangala hold, Actor-III can't bear it. Thus, he roars.]

Actor III   : Leave me.

Soma   : Gandhi is talking.

Actor III   : Scoundrels, you have come to take. (Beating them with the staff)

Mangala   : They groan in pain. Hey, Gandhi Baba! How can you beat it?

Actor III   : (Beating) Rascals-where are my *Gita* and goggles?

Mangala   : We don't have it right now. We have
               already sold them.

Actor III   : You don't have. Oh, I see!

               [Actor-III beats Rabi, Soma, and Mangala
               with the staff. They leave the place severely
               flagellated.]

Soma   : Gandhi has beaten us-

               [Actor-III runs after them, and the stage
               light is off. In the darkness, different voices
               are heard.]

Voice   : (In suppressed voice) Can you hear?
               Gandhi's Statue is infused with life. He is
               running after three thieves.

Voice   : (Slightly louder voice) Can you hear?
               Gandhi's Statue is infused with life. He is
               running after three thieves.

Voice   : (Loudly) Can you hear? Gandhi's Statue is
               infused with life. He is running after three
               thieves.

               [Announcement is heard immediately.]

Announcement: On behalf of newspapers, radio, television
               and the Public Relations Department, an
               announcement is made simultaneously,
               'You all maintain discipline in the city.' We
               are delighted that Gandhi is alive now on
               EarthEarth. He runs after some scoundrels to

give them a good lesson. The Police Department and C.B.I. Department are researching him now. The message will be public if the departments see Gandhi in the following news.

[There is light on stage. It's the Minister's house. Actor-I and Actor-II have come with the Minister.]

Actor I : What about Gandhi?

Minister : We will surely get it. Did you see what a big event this was? Many people inaugurated Gandhi's Statues; no statue was infused with life anywhere. As I inaugurated the Statue with my pure heart and holy soul, that would get life. Now, the whole world's eyes are on me. The high command of our party, being pleased with me on this event, will make me the Chief Minister.

Actor II : you may be the Chief Minister or Prime Minister. But where is our Gandhi?

Minister : Wherever Gandhi may be, what's your problem?

Actor I : That is our Gandhi.

Minister : How is your Gandhi? He is the National Property. Once he returns, he will kept in the museum. Or else he will be the secretary of our party. What's your problem?

Actor II   : We won't be returned or given back.

Minister   : No question arises. If you say like this, you
                will go to jail.

Actor II   : Sir, the way people are mad, you are also
                angry to run after them. How can a statue
                get a life?

Minister   : Why not? A few days before, Ganesh
                drank milk. Similarly, Gandhi got life.

Actor I   : What will you do with him?

Minister   : I will be the Chief Minister with his help.

Actor II   : You won't be given any posts. If Gandhi
                comes, he will be the Chief Minister.

Minister   : How will he be? Has he won any Member
                of the Legislative Assembly seats?

Actor I   : He may not win the election. If Gandhi had
                come, people would have been mad at him.
                The State Assembly will break down. He
                will win the election if he stands from any
                place. He had brought 'Independence' to our
                country. You will be nowhere.

Minister   : Will he be the candidate against me?

Actor I   : Absolutely. We will support him.

Minister : Then, It was a big mistake that Gandhi came. Why did he go if he had to stand in the election?

Actor II : We also think in the same line. Why is he here?

[Now Actor-I and Actor-II say as the announcers.]

Actor II : We collected fees in his name and spent away. Why did Gandhi come?

Actor I : We have opened *Gudakhu* (Tobacco mixed with molasses used for cleaning teeth) Shops, *Bidi* (Tobacco rolled up in a leaf used for smoking) Companies, and Shoe Stands in his name. Why did Gandhi come?

Minister : We have exploited our country politically in his name and ideology. Why did Gandhi come?

Actor II : Colour faded from his statue. Beside his statue, we reserved a place to take liquor and litter empty bottles. Why did Gandhi come?

Actor I : Having reached here, what will he see? He will see the ugly and vile nature lurking behind the coarse clothes.

Actor II : His established *Ram Rajya* (The state of truth and righteousness) is how he gets converted into *Ravan Rajya* (The state of falsehood, anarchy, and hypocrisy).

Actor I : Can Gandhi tolerate the communal riots, rivalry, bloodshed, and women's harassment?

Minister : Why has Gandhi come? He declared him the 'Father of the Nation'. Our parties continued in his name. We governed our country as per our needs. Will he stand again in the election?

Actor I : If Gandhi comes, the country's politics will change. The social picture of the nation will also change.

Actor II : Why will he come? He will suffer a lot. After fifty years of independence, the people of the country are still oppressed and dependent.

Actor I : This Gandhi is not that Gandhi. Gandhi is dead. Nobody can get life after death.

Minister : This man is somebody else in the name of Gandhi. He may be an extremist.

Actor II : He may be a conspirator to spread communal riots or casteism.

Minister : He may be a foreign agent to break down our country or a politician to form another political party.

Actor I   : I wonder whether Gandhi Statue gets life or something else.

Minister   : The Statue has not been infused with life. A computer is installed in it. The Foreign Companies have planned it. They are collecting secret information from our country. I have to inform the Department. There will be a question hour session in the Legislative Assembly. Whoever he may be, he should be arrested immediately.

Actor II   : Arrest-

Minister   : Yes, immediately-

Actor I   : Then our Gandhi Baba

Actor II   : "A great discovery from a small enquiry". Anyhow, we got our (I.e., fees of two thousand rupees).

[Miss Chandramukhi has come.]

Chandramukhi : Nay…

Minister   : Who?

Actor I   : Miss Chandramukhi

Actor II   : Mafia Don

Chandra   : Yes. Did you get your fees?

Actor I   : Yes, Miss.

Chandra   : How much?

Actor II   : Only two thousand

Chandra   : (To Actor-I) What about you?

Actor I   : Initially, we collected twelve thousand. We spent one thousand. The remaining amount was eleven thousand. We have received two thousand rupees from the Minister. In total, we have thirteen thousand.

Chandra   : A Cabinet Minister; to be a guest, he only pays fees of two thousand. What kind of Minister are you? You have sold trees and leaves; after all, you have sold the country. After swallowing all these, your belly is bulged out. But you are only paying two thousand in fees. Chandramukhi can't tolerate this injustice in her area. Number one!

Actor I   : Yes, Miss

Chandra   : Number two?

Actor II   : Yes, Miss

Chandra   : You titillate the Minister's waist. You will surely get fees.

Minister   : Chandramukhi, You don't send them. If you thrill me, I will give you another two thousand rupees.

Chandra   : I never step into a male person's shadow. I am the virgin Miss Chandramukhi. All of you surrender your fees collected.

Actor I   : Are you asking us, Miss?

Chandra   : Yes, to you all.

Actor II   : How will we live? We have collected fees throughout the month in the sun's searing heat. If you take all this, we will be nowhere.

Chandra   : I need that money.

Actor I   : Miss Chandramukhi, we will be utterly ruined.

Chandra   : Minister, you?

Minister   : I will give you, while you titillate me-

Chandra   : All denied to give. You Bastard! It would help if you had revenge (She brings out a knife.)

Minister   : What's this?

Chandra   : Rampuri pen-knife. I am with a pen-knife, and you are three. You are three to one knife. You three will die. How?

Minister   : Yes, how will we die?

Actor I   : We can't die.

Actor II   : Miss Chandramukhi is a good person.

Chandra   : You will die; how? I will stab one in the belly, one in the back and slit one's throat.

Actor I & II   : Don't kill us-

Chandra   : I need that money.

Actor I   : (Bringing out of his pocket) Take this

Chandra   : They all surrendered the money. (Laughing)

Actor II   : But, we are ruined now. We are penurious.

Chandra   : From Chandramukhi's hall, nobody returns empty-handed. I am pleased with you all. I will donate ten rupees to you daily to take the country's liquor.

Actors I & II   : Let's say, "Miss Chandramukhi Ki Jay!"

Chandra   : Shut up! Where is Gandhi?

Actor I   : We don't know.

Chandra   : You don't know? How can it be? I ask you, "Where is Gandhi?"

Actor II   : We are searching for him. He has been running after three scoundrels for the last three days.

Chandra   : Where has he gone? You need to figure out his whereabouts.

Minister   : Miss, why are you searching for Gandhi?

Chandra   : He is my Gandhi, the lord of my heart and my heart and soul. He is my darling, my love. I love him

Minister   : Then, you are Kasturba.

Chandra   : No, I am Mafia Don Miss Chandramukhi. One day, in my mind, a flower of love blossomed for him. He came and smelt the same. I withered like the touch-me-not plant (Mimosa Pudica). I clung to his body. But, today, rejecting my love, he runs after three rascals. I want to cry.

Minister   : Miss Chandramukhi's eyes are full of tears. Let Gandhi leave; I am here for you. You can think of me as 'Gandhi'.

Chandra   : What did you say?

Minister   : You blossom like a flower again. I will smell that flower. You will wither again like the touch-me-not plant-

Chandra   : Shut up. A dry *kendu* wood! You want to love me.

Minister   : Yes

Chandra   : Can you bear the pain?

Minister   : Pain?

Chandra : You have to bear pain after you own me. I will make you dance. You will dance until you die. But if you stop dancing, I will cut your legs with this knife.

Minister : What kind of love is it?

Chandra : After death, you will appear as a drumstick plant in my courtyard. I will eat that *saag* recipe in love.

Minister : Let my love stop here.

Chandra : Dance, but unrhythmically. If I find at any point in time any rhythm in your dance, my knife will kiss your feet. (To Actor-I & II) You titillate the Minister in his waist.

[Actor-I & Actor-II titillate the Minister.]

Minister : Well, I am dancing.

[One song is played on. When the Minister tries to dance, the stage light is off. After the stage light, a place on the city's outskirts is seen. After running for a while, Rabi, Soma, and Mangala are tired. Wounds are marked on their bodies. Rabi limps. Soma is serious. The clothes on Mangala's body are disrobed. Tired they are sitting at a place.]

Mangala : I have lost my energy. I can't run. I am exhausted. Gandhi has drained me up. I have denied you earlier. Because of you, I had to suffer.

Soma   : The interest in ganja at ten rupees has made me run ten miles.

Rabi   : Hello Brother! I limp with one of my legs. Gandhi has beaten me. Please save me. I can't run.

Mangala   : We can't hide anywhere. Gandhi reaches us, wherever we hide.

Rabi   : I have been hungry for the last three days. My legs swell, running for hours. I will die if you don't give me a glass of water.

Soma   : If I hide somewhere, this Gandhi won't allow me to live. Mangala- You do something.

Mangala   : What can I do?

Soma   : You try to stop Gandhi by any means. We start running.

Mangala   : What about me? If he sees us in the front, he beats us severely, and he breaks our hands and legs. I have pain in my back.

Rabi   : He searches for us every nook and corner. If he gets pleased by any means, but…

Soma   : I have an idea that I will research Gandhi. He will be happy.

Rabi

: Three days back, you had your ganja. You are still under its spell. Now, we think about how to save our lives. He says to do research.

Soma

: I have some secret information. The fact is that Gandhi didn't die in Nathuram Godse's bullets.

Mangala

: Didn't Gandhi die?

Soma

: He had visited the planet Mars on an aeroplane. He had been there till date. He was watching everything on Earth through the telescope.

Rabi

: He was alive.

Soma

: No, nobody dies on the planet Mars. Considering the overpopulation on Earth, he came down here to take some people with him.

Mangala

: Do the people live there?

Soma

: Yes. There, you will see metropolises like Kolkata, Delhi, Chennai, and Mumbai. People are wealthy there. They cultivate enough crops and cereals. They throw the rest into the sea. Everything is available there free of cost. One can see the ganja garden everywhere.

Mangala

: Yes, I will go there.

Soma	: How will you go? Gandhi is angry with you. But, I am researching on Gandhi. Being pleased he will take me with him. Gandhi was, in fact, not dead. After my research work is published, the history books will be proven wrong. Those who have installed his Statue and are celebrating his 'Birth Anniversary' will be sent to jail; for this, Gandhi will be happy with me.
Rabi	: Then, why is Gandhi angry with us?
Soma	: We took ganja selling his goggles and *Gita*. We told them that he was dead. That's why he was angry. Now, I have written a poem on him. Can I read it out? He won't flog me. (He is reading the poem.)

"Gandhi is not dead and won't die on this world stage,

   All others will die, after their works, under Gandhi's spell."

Mangala	: I will surrender at his feet. I will confess all my crimes before him. He will pardon me.
Rabi	: I will say, "Oh, Gandhi Mahatma! I am a mean person. I have committed many crimes in my life for my stomach. I will never commit any crime. I will never use any filthy words. I will never see anything wrong. "

Soma   : We all will surrender before him. We will
                  sing the National Anthem before him.
                  Mangala, remember this.

Mangala   : Yes.

Soma   : Please be seated peacefully. Gandhi is
                  coming.

Mangala   : Nay, he will beat me. I am leaving the
                  place.

Rabi   : Shut up! [Rabi, Soma and Mangla are
                  sitting like Gandhi's three monkeys. Actor-
                  III reaches there searching for them.]

Actor III   : Where are they?

All   : We are here.

Actor III   : What are you doing here?

Rabi   : We will appreciate your attributes. We
                  have been your three monkeys.

Soma   : We won't see anything wrong.

Rabi/Mangala : Mahatma Gandhi Ki Jay!

Soma   : We won't say anything wrong.

Rabi/Mangala : Mahatma Gandhi Ki Jay!

Soma   : We won't do anything wrong.

Rabi/Mangala : Mahatma Gandhi Ki Jay!

Actor III   : Where are my *Gita* and goggles?

Rabi/Soma/Mangala : We sold in the market.

Soma   : Please pardon us. Bring back from them whom you have sold.

Mangala   : We will avoid repeating the same mistake.

Actor III   : No-

Soma   : Gandhi Baba, you are very compassionate and a kind-hearted person. I love a girl. I gave her a dress and a bunch of bangles and fed her *dahi-bara*. She must have been searching for me since the day you ran after us. She must be in sorrow not seeing me long. She will run away with somebody else if I don't reach her in time. You can save my love, Gandhi Baba.

Mangala   : Gandhibaba, though I am the father of seven children, my wife can't stay alone for a moment without me. This is because I have an extramarital relationship with three women. She must be searching for me in my absence. She will suspect me. After that, she will take poison. Four times, she has taken poison. She is still alive. She may die this time. Please pardon me.

Rabi   : Gandhi Baba- After forty years of my bachelor life, six months before my luck favours me. I have visited Cuttack, Puri, and Balasore for forty years. I have been harassed. Now, I am fully mad in my wife's love. You can pardon me. I am burnt in pangs of separation.

All   : (Prostrating before Actor-III) We confess our mistakes. Please pardon us.

Actor III   : "A sheep in wolf's clothing" [He beats Mangala with his staff.]

Rabi/Soma/Mangala : *"raghupati rāgham rājārām, patitapāban sitārām,*

īśwar āllah tere nām, sabko sanmati de bhagbān."

[They are singing around Actor III.]

Actor III   : Where is my *Gita*?

Rabi   : We have sold.

Actor III   : Where is my spectacle?

Soma   : We have sold.

Actor III   : Why?

Mangala   : We smoked ganja. We have made mistakes. We swear we won't repeat the same for my mother's and father's sake. You are our 'Father of the Nation'. Before you, we promise not to take ganja anymore.

Actor III : All right. Well, say who I am?

Rabi : You are Ga…n...dhi…You're Gandhi.

Soma : You are Ga…n...dhi…You're Gandhi.

Mangala : You are Ga…ndhi…You're Gandhi.

Actor III : No…I am not Gandhi. I am Ramdas, a hooligan of this city. I am acting in Gandhi's role. As my acting and character coincide, I am Gandhi. So, I am a Gandhi.

Rabi/Soma/Mangala : *Gandhi Baba Ki Jay*!

Actor III : Where is my bundle of ganja?

Mangala : Sir, have you kept? Please give us. I am exhausted. My body aches. Let me take a sip of ganja.

Rabi : Please, give us. Our mouth dries up.

Actor III : Ok. I am giving you all, you scoundrel, the herd addicted to smoking ganja.

[He is chasing with his staff. Rabi, Soma, and Mangala are running. A police whistle is heard behind. The stage light is off. After the light, a Police Station is seen. Rabi, Soma, and Mangal stand on one side, while

Actor III stands on the other. A Police Inspector strolls in their front.]

Inspector   : Who are you all?

Rabi   : We are Rabi, Soma, and Mangala. We write poems and do research.

Inspector   : Why did Gandhi Baba chase you all?

Soma   : We have not committed any crime. But we have sold Gandhi's *Gita* and goggles in the market.

Inspector   : How did you sell '*Gita*'?

Mangala   : We have made a mistake, Sir. We don't have money to buy ganja.

Inspector   : Only that or something else.

Rabi   : No-we had planned to steal his statue. Then Gandhi getting life chased us.

Inspector   : Were you stealing?

Soma   : We have not stolen. We are going to steal.

Inspector   : How is your body with the scars and wounds?

Mangala   : Gandhi Baba thrashed us. To save our lives, we fought. This is the consequence.

Inspector   : You have disrespected the 'Father of the Nation'. You will be imprisoned.

Mangala	: Sir, after all, he is not the Gandhi.
Inspector	: How did you know?
Rabi	: Gandhi was very lean and thin. We, three, could not fight with him.
Soma	: Gandhi didn't know Odia. How does he speak Odia?
Mangala	: Gandhi believes in non-violence. He has beaten us with his staff.
Rabi	: He is not Gandhi at all.
Inspector	: I will look into the matter. Enter the jail now.
Rabi	: Our fault?
Inspector	: You have stolen and sold his goggles and *Gita*. You have squabbled over trivial matters. Enter the jail. [The Inspector is pushing them into the prison.]
Mangala	: We are in jail unnecessarily.

[Rabi, Soma and Mangala are inside the jail. Now the Inspector comes to Actor-III.]

Inspector	: Who are you?
Actor III	: Gandhi
Inspector	: Speak the truth. Who are you?

Actor III   : I am an actor. I am acting in Gandhi's role. What has happened until now was all my acting.

Inspector   : You can't act any more.

Actor III   : There won't be any need of acting. My real life has been mingled with this role of Gandhi.

Inspector   : Who are you?

Actor III   : I am Ramdas, a hooligan of *Golei Chowk*.

Inspector   : Ramdas- Are you in Gandhi's role?

Actor III   : I was searching for a way to be a gentleman. I have found it now.

Inspector   : No one can pardon you for the crime you have committed. You have insulted 'Father of the Nation'.

Actor III   : I have sinned but have not disrespected him. I was involved in evil or antisocial activities and hooliganism. Some days, we had heavy collections, and some days, we didn't get anything to eat. In Gandhi's, we collected twelve thousand rupees to distribute among ourselves equally. That's why I became Gandhi.

Inspector   : You are confessing the guilty.

Actor III : Let me speak, Inspector. I have never had peace in life. The time I have spent in Gandhi's role has given me peace. People respect me. I earn pleasure in pain while I stand as Gandhi somewhere for long. That time, I have not thought of anything evil, not moved on the wrong path, and not deprived anyone of his rights. I have spent that time as a gentleman. I have also got peace.

Inspector : So, you will go to jail.

Actor III : My fault/crime?

Inspector : You had cheated others twelve thousand rupees in Gandhi's name.

Actor III : In this country, the politicians cheat crores and crores of rupees. What type of jail do you have for them?

Inspector : I am not forcing you to reply to that.

Actor III : Inspector Sir, I want to lead a life as honest as Gandhi. I will change the path of my life. Let me live.

Inspector : That's not possible. Go to jail.

Actor III : Is living like Gandhi in the world a crime?

Inspector : Don't talk nonsense. [Minister hears all this a few minutes before. He interferes there.]

Minister   : Please, release him, Inspector.

Inspector   : Sir, *Namaskar!*

Minister   : *Namaskar*, I am with the 'Bail Order' from
                the court for him. You see [He shows the
                letter.]

Inspector   : When you have brought, I must release
                him. But this person won't be helpful to you
                at all.

Minister   : I have to serve the nation when I am the
                minister. Let's assume this is one of my
                social works. You can go now.

Inspector   : I leave now, Sir! *Namaskar!*

Minister   : *Namaskar*! [Inspector leaves.]

Minister   : Then you are not Gandhi.

Actor III   : No-

Minister   : Are you acting in Gandhi's role?

Actor III   : Yes-

Minister   : I thought of that while inaugurating the
                statue. Later, I thought, you looked at me so
                under the spell of my intoxication. If you are
                not Gandhi, then who are you?

Actor III   : I am Ramdas of *Golei Chowk.*

Minister   : You, Gandhi?

Actor III   : Yes, Bandit Ratnakar can also be Valmiki.

Minister   : All right. Do you want to live like Gandhi?

Actor III   : Can you allow me to live?

Minister   : For that, I have taken you on bail.

Actor III   : Thank you so much!

Minister   : You have to work with me.

Actor III   : What sort of work?

Minister   : You will be in this Gandhi dress throughout your life. You will ask for votes for me in the meetings. You will reach people. You will work for our party. Gandhi was also doing this. I will give you thirty rupees per day.

Actor III   : Anything else other than that?

Minister   : No-

Actor III   : All right. What are the situations that Gandhi underwent in the twentieth century?

Minister   : Join our party tomorrow.

Actor III   : Sir [Actor III says 'pranam' to the Minister. Both of them move in opposite directions. At that time, Actor-I and Actor-II come from opposite directions.]

Actor I   : Sir, *Namaskar*! The next step of the story starts from here. Subsequently, Actor I and Actor II, ceasing earlier roles, act as the announcers.

Actor II   : In this part, all actors change their characters.

Actor I   : Promising before the minister, Ramdas becomes Gandhi for his entire life. Gradually, his outer getup has influenced his soul. Early in the morning, he reads Gandhi, weaves thread through the spinning wheel, and wears coarse garments. His lifestyle gets changed in due course.

Actor II   : The second part of the story is about Ramdas's hectic life schedule in Gandhi's role.

Actor I   : Ramdas in Gandhi dress wanders daily from morning to evening. He stands as Gandhi in every Birth Anniversary of Gandhi. He campaigns for a vote and returns to the minister in the evening for thirty rupees.

Actor II   : Perhaps Ramdas is coming to the Minister

[Actor-I and Actor-II move in different directions. Ramdas has come tired.]

Actor III   : Is Sir at home? [The undergarments of a woman are thrown to his face.]

Actor III   : Is Sir at home? [An empty wine bottle comes rolling.]

Actor III   : Is Sir at home? [The minister comes unsteady.]

Minister   : What happened?

Actor III   : I have come to take my money.

Minister   : I am in trouble. Come tomorrow to receive your money.

Actor III   : You have been saying so since the month started. What can I eat?

Minister   : I have already told you to come and receive the amount tomorrow. Don't irritate me. Leave this place.

Actor III   : Please listen to me.

Minister   : What?

Actor III   : If I return empty-handed, I will have nothing to eat tonight.

Minister   : What shall I do? Will I feed you? What have you done for the month?

Actor III   : You ordered me to wander from village to village, requesting to vote in your favour. While walking from place to place, sometimes I ate a bowl of flattened rice, drank a bottle of water, sometimes slept on someone's verandah and sometimes spent a night under the tree. I have told people to vote for you. I have done what you said.

Minister : OK, I will consider your matter later. I can't pay you now.

Actor III : I urgently need money. I had not taken food for the last two days.

Minister : I am telling the priest that he will give you food. You will have it.

Actor III : No. I don't beg anybody to eat. Once upon a time, I had no deficit of money. I was not borrowing from anybody. I was forcefully snatching. All were afraid of me. But today, to be a gentleman, I am suffering. All are saying that this is my madness. I also think this is my madness. If one becomes a gentleman, what will he get? Is it love, respect, prestige, affection and self-reliance? I am still waiting to receive something. Everything reverses in my case. Still, I can't be Ramdas. Though it is hard to live, I love this life.

Minister : Is it so?

Actor III : At the time of having camps in the villages, when you were relishing fish and chicken curries and sleeping in the bungalows, I was sleeping in someone's verandah eating a bowl of uncooked flattened rice. I think of only one thing: how people use me in Gandhi's attire. Had Mahatma Gandhi been here, how would he have suffered in the present time?

Minister : How would I allow a vagabond and hooligan of the slum to sit on the bedstead?

Actor III : You are right. You always allow the hooligans like Ramdas to sit on your bedstead, but today, you dislike Ramdas in Gandhi's dress.

Minister : Being a servant of thirty rupees, you are teaching me.

Actor III : What did you say?

Minister : Couldn't you hear?

Actor III : Yes, I heard. Please remember, I have not become Gandhi to be a servant. I struggle hard to be recognized as a gentleman in society. You give me thirty rupees, not because of sympathy, but the value of my labour. If you think of me as your servant, I only quit this job today.

Minister : Ok. Go away from me right now. I don't need the persons like you.

Actor III : My payment?

Minister : I won't give you anything. [Minister leaves the place out of anger.]

Actor III   : It's OK. As you wish-

[Actor-III leaves the place silently. Actor-I and Actor-II are coming from two sides.]

The actor I , Ramdas, becomes silent as the photos of Gandhi hang in the Minister's bedroom. He returns peacefully. He has nothing to eat at home. Drinking a glass of water, he sleeps.

Actor II   : No one can discover why Ramdas lives such a life. He has to pay the rent for the house where he used to stay with respect. At last, the owner drove him away from the house. The shopkeepers who used to give tips before denied him the ability to sell anything in credit. Those who were afraid of him earlier laughed at him and joked. Ramdas was leading an insulted life.

Actor I   : He searches for a new job. The next day, he meets a businessman.

Actor II   : Let's assume a businessman is coming before us.

[These two go to the sides of the stage and become silent. Then Actor-III and Rabi (Businessman) come from opposite directions.]

Actor III   : Lalaji-*Namaskar*!

Rabi   : Yes, I remember you. I hear that you have left the job at the minister's house.

Actor III   : Yes.

Rabi   : Can you work with us?

Actor III   : What's the work?

Rabi   : We have launched a new type of coarse sari. It needs to be advertised. You will stand in our showcase all day wearing this coarse sari. We will get some benefits, and you will take your payment.

Actor III   : Whole day inside the showcase?

Rabi   : Yes, until the shop gets closed. People will watch you. You will do our sari's advertisement.

Actor III   : How much will I get?

Rabi   : Twenty-five rupees per day.

Actor III   : Only twenty-five rupees-

Rabi   : You will draw a monthly salary of seven hundred and fifty rupees. Who will pay you this amount freely without any work? You will stand up only. We are also not earning that amount working for the entire month. It depends on you. If you like, you can come. Otherwise, no need to go here.

Actor III   : Is the value of Gandhi only Rs. 750/-
              (Seven Hundred and Fifty Rupees)?

Rabi   : Why are you talking of Gandhi? You are
              the original Gandhi. Do you need to do
              business wearing his dress?

Actor III   : I am doing business to live a better life.

Rabi   : We are also doing business to live. No
              further discussion. A simple question to you
              is whether you will work or not.

Actor III   : There is no other option to live. Let me
              take this chance. Lalaji- I agree with your
              proposal.

Rabi   : Come tomorrow to join the work.

Actor III   : Yes-

              [Rabi and Actor-III go away in opposite
              directions. Actor-I and Actor-II come to the
              audience from the front side.]

Actor I   : From 6 a.m. to midnight, Ramdas stands
              up in the showcase in a Gandhi dress. He
              feels pain in his legs. The customers come
              and return purchasing saris. At midnight, he
              returns home exhausted. But his struggle to
              live does not end here.

Actor II   : At the end of the month, when he requests
              his salary, he gets the answer that they have

no good business this month. Next month you will be paid.

Actor I : Ramdas searches for a job in hunger and anxiety. He quests for a way to live. He meets a film producer accidentally.

Actor II : Let's assume that the Film Producer is in the front.

[Actor-I and Actor-II go to two sides of the stage and become silent. Actor-III and Soma come from the inside. Soma is the Film Producer now.]

Soma : Are you Ramdas?

Actor-III : Yes, Sir.

Soma : When I saw you, I thought of you so. You look exactly like Gandhi. I am Subash Nanda, Film Producer.

Actor III : You are working in the film line. Do you have any work with me?

Soma : Yes, I have. I will tell you later. What are you doing nowadays?

Actor III : Nothing. I am unemployed.

Soma : Are you interested in working with me?

Actor III : I have no faith in work. I have been cheated twice.

Soma   : Don't think of all alike. Nobody gets deceived at my workplace. Are you interested in working?

Actor III   : What to do?

Soma   : You will act in the role of Gandhi in Advertisement Film.

Actor III   : I don't know how to act.

Soma   : We will train you that. Don't worry.

Actor III   : All right. But will I get my payment right?

Soma   : You can receive the whole amount in advance.

Actor III   : I don't need the total amount. I need the price of my labour.

Soma   : You will get that in time. You can join the work tomorrow. I will be waiting for you at Sakharam Studio at 10.00 AM.

Actor III   : Yes, Sir!

[Actor-III and Soma, moving in two different directions, stay silent there. Actor-I and Actor-II now come to the front of the stage.]

Actor I   : Initially, Ramdas liked the work in Film Industry. But later, he got disheartened and perplexed by the shocking and appalling scenes of the world.

Actor II   : He quarrelled with the Producer for their different opinions.

Actor I   : Ramdas thought those using him for Gandhi's role would respect some shows on Gandhi. But everybody engaged him in their spheres from a business point of view.

Actor II   : There were often fights between Ramdas's Gandhian Philosophy and others' business-centric approach. He was getting neither respect nor the price of his work anywhere. With this mental tension, he couldn't work anywhere. After all, he was not satisfied.

Actor I   : Ramdas said, 'He can bear insult showered on him, but not upon the Gandhi dress.' He coincided with Gandhi's role, so it was tough for him to segregate.

Actor II   : As a result, he was forced to give up the Film Industry.

[Actor-I and Actor-II stay silently on two sides of the stage. Soma, the film producer, comes to the front.]

Soma   : What nonsense are you talking of? You have misbehaved, my heroine.

Actor III   : Yes-

Soma   : Why?

Actor III   : She misbehaved with me, telling me to drop her in her car.

Soma   : What's wrong with that?

Actor III   : Gandhi can't bear this kind of obscenity.

Soma   : But you are not Gandhi. Like you, many people have acted in Gandhi's role. Acting is not the real life.

Actor III   : But I have mingled my acting with real life.

Soma   : For you, many problems arise. That day, you denied drinking at the Pool Party.

Actor III   : I have given up drinking.

Soma   : This is the etiquette of our industry.

Actor III   : I can't be forced to obey that decorum.

Soma   : I am not forced to tolerate the problems arising in the industry for you. You can only adjust with yourself. After all, you are a junior artist.

Actor III   : I am not an artist, but Gandhi.

Soma   : You are not Gandhi. If you have no interest in working, you can give up the film line and go to hell.

Actor III   : I quit the job now.

Soma   : What did you say? You are a junior artist in my unit. How can you say so? If I remove you from my unit, nobody in the Film Industry will look at your face. You will wander begging alms from door to door in the society.

Actor III   : Hey, Producer! Don't try to wake up repeatedly the Ramdas sleeping under the guise of Gandhi. Please don't force me to step out into society with a dagger. I have erased all this from my mind. Go and do your work. I will take care of my life.

Soma   : All right. Then, go to hell.

[Soma leaves.]

Actor III   : All are businessmen. To live as a gentleman here is very difficult.

[Actor-III is extremely unhappy and helpless. While returning, Mangala, a follower of the Minister, meets him and stops.]

Mangala   : Are you Ramdas?

Actor III   : Yes-

Mangala   : I am P. A. to the Minister. Please, come with me.

Actor III   : Where?

Mangala   : To the Minister

Actor III   : I have given up my job there. Now I can't
              go anywhere.

Mangala   : The Minister has said, "I have to take you
              at any cost."

Actor III   : Why?

Mangala   : A few days are left for the Election. You
              have to campaign for the Minister.

Actor III   : Go to tell him that Ramdas has denied it.

Mangala   : All right. I will tell him. But do you know
              what your condition will be?

Actor III   : Are you threatening me?

Mangala   : Your name is for the welfare of the public.
              Can you remember the day when you were
              chasing three ruffians, and the Police
              arrested you? You would have gone to jail.
              But before that, the Minister took you on
              bail. Ramdas, you are, to date, the Minister's
              trust or people. If you disagree with this
              proposal, the Police may issue a 'Warrant
              Order' against your name anytime. The case
              will continue. Maybe you will be in jail.

Actor III   : What did you say?

Mangala   : Do you like to spend your entire life inside
               jail?

Actor III   : I understood that the Minister would like to
               blackmail me. Well, what do I have to do for
               the minister?

Mangala   : You will distribute money to the voters in
               the Election.

Actor III   : I?

Mangala   : Who is safer and more secure than you in
               society? Nobody will doubt you. You will
               give away money among the people, and the
               minister will get votes and win the Election.

Actor III   : (Shouting) Bastard! (Holding Mangala's
               neck)

Mangala   : Hey, why are you holding my neck? Leave
               me, or else we will take action against you.

Actor III   : What do you think? Is Ramdas a eunuch?
               Is he a rubber toy that will dance as per your
               instructions? Everyone was afraid of me
               when I was coming out with a dagger.

Mangala   : Please leave my neck.

Actor III   : I will squeeze your throat.

Mangala   : Ah, save me [Actor-I and Actor-II from in
               the front say.]

Actor I   : Ramdas-what are you doing? Leave him-

Actor II   : Being Gandhi, are you going to kill a man?

               [Ramdas is conscious of the situation and releases Mangala from his clutch.]

Actor III   : What am I going to be? Gandhi or Ramdas?

Mangala   : OK, I will see you. (He runs from there.)

Actor III   : What am I going to be? Gandhi or Ramdas? Gandhi or Ramdas? No-no-

               [Ramdas (Actor-III) runs breathlessly. Then, the stage is lit off. After the stage light, Ramdas is seen at his home. He enters his home after running breathlessly. He stands holding the fence of the wall.]

Actor III   : What am I going to be? Gandhi or Ramdas?

               [Then Rabi, Soma and Mangala come to his residence. It's the reflection of Ramdas's subconscious mind. They are revolving around Actor-III.]

Rabi   : Hi-Ramdas!

Soma   : Hi!

Mangala   : Ramdas!

Rabi   : What are you doing?

[Ramdas looks at them helplessly.]

Actor III : I am trying to live.

Rabi : Do you want to live like a wooden toy in my showcase with a salary of fifty rupees per month?

Soma : If I drive away from the Film Industry, you will be useless. No one will look at you. You will wander begging from door to door.

Mangala : You are an ordinary servant of the minister. Will you work or go to jail?

Rabi : Ramdas

Soma : Will you work?

Mangala : Or else go to jail.

[This voice is repeatedly echoed. Actor-III cries out in tension.]

Actor III : No…no…no

[After shouting, he sits silently. Rabi, Soma and Mangal leave the place gradually. Ramadas's mind has a storm of conflict for either creation or destruction. Maybe Ramdas emerges from him. Everywhere is the musical rhythm of *Shiv Tandav Strotam*, as if Shiv came out in that storm for his dance.]

A song is heard:

Sanskrit   : *"jaṭāṭavigaljjala pravāhpāvitasthale*

    galeavalambya   lambitāṁ bhujaṅgatuṅgmālikām

    ḍamaḍ   ḍamaḍ   ḍamaḍ   ḍama ninādavaddamarvayaṁ,

    chakār chaṇḍtāṇḍavaṁ tanotunah śivah śivam."

English   : "With his neck consecrated by the flow of water that flows from his hair,

    And on his neck, a snake is hung like a garland.

    And the Damaru drum that emits the sound 'Damat Damat Damat Damat.'

    Shiva did the auspicious dance of Tandava to bring us prosperity."

[Different lights are changed continuously with sound on the stage to create a storm effect in people's minds. Actor-II shows different poses through his different gestures.]

Sanskrit   :   *"jatā   katāhsambhrama
bhramannilimpanirjhari,*

vilolavichiballari virājamānamurddhani,

*dhagadhagadhagajjvalallalāta   patta
pāvake,*

*kiśorachandraśekhare ratih pratikshanam
mamam."*

English   : "I have a deep interest in Lord Shiva,
whose head is glorified by the propagating
waves of the celestial Ganga River,

That stirs in the deep well of his hair in
tangled locks;

On the surface of whose forehead the
brilliant fire is burning,

And who has the crescent moon as a jewel
on his head."

[A few minutes before reaching
Chandramukhi here, he watches all this
silently. She can't bear such a fall of Ramdas
in the front. She thinks Ramdas has lost his
prestige and dignity. So, she bursts out her
anger. After the Tandava Dance ends, when
Ramdas falls on the ground, Chandramukhi
beats him cruelly.]

Chandramukhi: You bastard, get up. Get up!

[Actor-III can't wake up in pain. Chandramukhi helps him get up.]

Chandramukhi: You will be Gandhi for an hour. People will salute you. Ramdas's character will be hidden and forgotten. You will be a gentleman.

Actor III : (Groaning) Ah!

Chandra : Deceived in love from you, this Chandramukhi has returned insulted. (I have beaten you out of anger.) you are begging alms before the minister. You are standing like a peon in the Businessman's showcase. You are playing the role of an eunuch in the cinema. Are you a male? One day, people were afraid of him. But today, you are an eunuch. Go to hell.

[Chandramukhi sits in anger and anguish. Ramdas is at a distance from her.]

Chandra : Go to hell (Her self-esteem and repressed anger come out. She is beating her hand on the ground because he has beaten him. At last, she cries. Ramdas is silent. Silence persists between the two for some time.)

Chandra : I once told you a jackal, being coloured in blue, became a king. But the day its nature was revealed, nobody accepted the jackal. Say whether I told you or not.

Actor III   : (Silent)

Chandra   : You are the Arjun of my love. Because of
                you, Chandramukhi walked on the road with
                pomp and vigour. She had loved you. But
                today, you are a mouse.

Actor III   : (Silent)

Chandra   : Oye, why are you not saying anything?

Actor III   : (Silent)

Chandramukhi: What will you say? You say I hate you.
                You will push me out of your home. I am an
                unlettered fellow, shameless, and a girl
                possessing masculine behaviour. I don't
                have any quality to be a bride. [Ramdas
                stands up slowly.]

Actor III   : Chandramukhi [She comes running to
                him.]

Chandra   : Are you calling me?

Actor III   : Water-[Chandramukhi go to the water pot
                and bring him a glass of water.]

Chandra   : Take water-

Actor III   : (Drinking) Thank you, Chandramukhi

Chandra   : Thanks? To me? No, Ramdas, I have
                beaten you a lot. Why are you saying 'thank
                you' to me?

Actor III : Thank you, Chandramukhi! I am a Gandhi. You saved me before I was converted to Ramdas.

Chandra : No- I have beaten you. I couldn't suppress my anger. You correctly said, 'I don't have any quality of a bride.'

Actor III : Gandhi said, 'If anybody slaps your left cheek, show your right cheek to him.' You see, how a person understands her mistake after beating a lot to someone.

Chandra : (getting startled) Please pardon me, Ramdas.

Actor III : I am an ordinary person. If you confess your mistake, God will forgive you.

Chandra : Today, you seem to be God to me.

Actor III : (Smiling)

Chandra : Ramdas!!

Actor III : No...Gandhi. Ramdas can't sit silently after being beaten. But, Gandhi, being shot the bullets, remained silent.

Chandra : You know so much but can't win my heart.

Actor III : Forcibly, nobody can win others' minds. The real victory is to win one's heart.

Chandra : (Silent)

Actor III : Chandramukhi! People are afraid of us. They don't love us. By snatching food from others, we live comfortably. Try to eat *ragi* (finger millet) gruel at least once with your hard work. You will get peace in that.

Chandra : (Silent)

Actor III : Chandramukhi, the God within me and under whose spell Ramdas can be changed into Gandhi, is also within you. In our sinful tendency, godly nature is hidden. Let it be expressed.

Chandra : Following this path, you are suffering and want me to suffer. Like you, I can't beg before the minister. I can't stand in the show Case of the Businessman. I can't be an eunuch in the cinema. I can't suffer like you.

Actor III : You love me, and for my love's sake, can you not do this? (Chandramukhi gets startled in silence.) Right, Chandramukhi, Is there love without body? I suffer in my way. Try to live in your way.

[When Actor-III leaves the place silently, chandramukhi calls him.]

Chandra : Gandhi (Ramdas looks at her and takes a turn. Chandramukhi is near him.)

Actor III : Chandramukhi

Chandra : Is it the right path?

Actor III : What you ask me today also lies in others' minds. Why has Ramdas been suddenly changed? Why has Ramdas, giving up his respect and influence, strength of arms, and lust for money, led to a very oppressed and insulting life in society?

Chandra : Why Ramdas? Why?

Actor III : The day I was born, my father didn't give me my father's identity. My mother, hungry for seven days in his courtyard, came to the town. The town is a wild city. To save my life, she had sacrificed her body repeatedly in this city. When I was mature and grown up, I saw how my mother was raped by the so-called wealthy and affluent people in the town. Now, I can also remember her tears and cries. One day, she died of cancer. When the sweeper threw her body, everybody was saying, 'It was good that a prostitute died at last.' From that day onwards, my identity was in crisis. Others treat me as a bastard. That bastard child becomes the Bandit Ramdas in due course.

Chandra : Ramdas!

Actor III : I have shown my hooliganism, murdered people, and snatched money from people. Later, I realized I had been the right-hand man to those who were the most wanted culprits in the city. The politicians have used me as their weapon. My target was only the innocent people. Here, my life has been full of dangers. The ruffians' daggers were after me, and so were the police's bullets. I can't sleep at night because of my illegal means of income. Life becomes uncertain. I spent hours in Gandhi's role at one stage of my life. The peace I found at that moment was something I had never experienced in my life. I forgot everything. Who am I? What's my identity?

[Chandramukhi suddenly sits at his feet and surrenders the knives from her pockets.]

Actor III   : Chandramukhi?

Chandra   : Can I not walk on your way?

[Ramdas embraces Chandramukhi in love and affection. He holds her hands, and both march on an unending path.]

Actor III   : Come with me-

[When they are moving ahead, the ringing of the wedding bell is heard on the soundtrack. They are lost in the backstage. Actor-I and Actor-II come to the front stage.]

Actor I   : Ramdas married Chandramukhi.

Actor II: After the marriage, Ramdas's responsibility increased.

Actor I   : He is financially weak to maintain the family.

Actor II   : He has no income. He does not have a thatched house to live in. At this critical moment, he engaged himself in two or three works. All tried to exploit him.

The actor I   : Nobody pays him his due, right? He couldn't adjust himself to anybody. At last, he thought living honestly in this world was challenging.

Actor II   : His wife was admitted to the hospital for her illness. Ramdas was sitting unhappily without getting money from anybody. His old friends Viki and Sunny met him.

[Actor-I and Actor-II, doing the roles of Viki and Sunny, comes to Actor-III.].

Actor I : Ramdas?

Actor III : Viki and Sunny! How are you?

Actor II : We came to see what you are doing.

Actor III : I am reading *Gita*.

Actor I : *Gita*?

Actor III : Chandramukhi's health is critical, and admitted to the hospital. I need money to purchase medicines. Evil thoughts come to my mind. That's why I am reading *Gita*.

Actor II : If you read *Gita*, will Chandramukhi recover from her illness?

Actor III : Then you get peace of mind. I pray to God. He will help me.

Actor I : Can God give you money? Listen to me, Ramdas. Give up this lunacy. We were born evil persons in the world. One way for us is to engage ourselves in wicked works. Nobody will believe us if we try to live as gentlemen. They won't help us. Instead, they will laugh at us and extend their sympathy to us.

Actor II : Will society allow us to live if we hold *Gita* in our hands instead of knives and daggers? It's wrong. In many places, you have surrendered before people to live honestly. What happened? Could you stay anywhere? Ramdas, for us, the only way to live is pickpocketing, selling cinema tickets in black and hooliganism. An honest person lives here with many difficulties.

Actor III : No, the way I have chosen is the life's truth. Don't request that I return from there.

Actor I : Ramadas, when you were practising hooliganism, earning money, and engaging yourself in entertainment, people were afraid of you. But when you started roaming, wearing coarse clothes, holding Gita in your hands, seeing your poverty all left you and your sick wife was hospitalized. You can't purchase medicines for her. Now say, do you like to live like this.

Actor II : Come back and join us, Ramdas! We have the road before us. We won't be empty-bellied once we step out with a dagger. You will receive insults and contempt, not money if you beg others.

Actor III : No. Give me a chance to live as a gentleman. I still think there is something 'truth' in this world. There is some value in an ideal. I have not lost my faith. Let me examine myself at least once. If defeated, then Ramdas will get down to the streets.

[Actor-III slowly leaves the place. Actor-I and Actor-II come to the front stage to face the audience from there.]

Actor I : Ramdas lived life with this kind of faith.

Actor II   : His wife is in the medical. He does not have money.

Actor I   : In the next stage of the story, Ramdas wanders everywhere for his wife's treatment. But nobody gave him any job.

Actor II   : At last, he knocked on the minister's door. The minister ordered him to work for the party. There was the Chairman's Election. He was sent to the hilly area to campaign in the Election to request that the voters cast their vote with folding palms for their candidate. He will be paid twenty-five rupees per day. Ramdas agreed to the proposal at this critical moment. Earlier, it was tough for him to find a job with the stamp of a ruffian.

Actor I   : Ramdas stayed for twenty days in the hilly area campaigning in the election.

Actor II   : Unfortunately, the Minister's candidate was defeated in the Election. At that time, Ramdas reached the Minister for his payment he would do his wife's treatment.

[Actor-I and Actor-II move in opposite directions. The stage light is off. It is the Minister's bungalow. The minister was strolling, disturbed. He enters the room to bring a glass of wine and drinks. Rabi, Soma and Mangala are with him.]

Minister   : defeated- my candidate got defeated in the Election. I gave away the clothes. Walking on the clay road, I requested the people with folding palms. I defeated. I have been nowhere. I will take revenge upon them. I will ruin them. (Rabi, Soma and Mangala) What were you all doing?

Rabi : Winning and losing in the Election is a common event.

Soma : Why are you so worried?

Mangala : You are one of many who have spent money. We have also spent money on the Election.

Minister : I am ruined.

Rabi : Please have patience.

Minister : My candidate was defeated. [Chandramukhi comes.]

Chandramukhi: Is the Honorable Minister at home?

Minister : Mafia Don Miss Chandramukhi. Why are you here?

Chandra : I am searching for him.

Minister : Who do you search for?

Chandra : My Gandhi

Minister : Gandhi is in the heavenly abode.

Chandra : Don't talk nonsense. You have sent him outside to campaign in the election for the last twenty days. He has yet to return.

Minister : You are talking of Ramdas. What will he be to you?

Chandra   : I am his wife.

Minister   : We told you much. You didn't listen to us.
               At last, you got married to Ramdas.

Chandra   : Hello, Minister! Hold your tongue.

Minister   : Have you yet to bring the pen knife with
               you?

Chandra   : You are fortunate. I have promised Ramdas
               not to involve myself in any antisocial work.
               I won't use that. Otherwise, I could have
               beheaded you.

Minister   : Then, it was good. You will be helpful to
               us.

Chandra   : What do you mean?

Rabi   : I mean to say you are lovely.

Soma   : She is an untamed myna.

Mangala   : The untamed myna can fly well.

Minister   : Then we will allow her to fly. Time is
               propitious.

               [Chandramukhi prepares herself to leave the
               place in apprehension.]

Chandra   : I leave now. You will pass the information
               to him that your wife is unwell. The doctor
               has scheduled a date for the operation. He
               will reach me soon. [When Chandramukhi
               was leaving, these people gheraoed her like
               the predators.]

Minister   : He won't come.

Chandra   : What?

Rabi   : The minister won't take him on bail if he
               comes. He will go to jail.

Soma   : Because of him, our party was defeated.

Mangala   : So, we won't allow him to work here.

Chandra   : All right! You will tell him to come
               immediately.

Minister   : Where are you going?

Chandra   : To my home

Rabi   : Well, this is the night. We will have a 'play
               rehearsal' here tonight. You can do a role
               for us.

Chandra   : Why are you talking nonsense?

Soma   : No, we will do the 'Play of Disrobing' in
               the Mahabharat. You can do Draupadi's
               role.

               [Rabi, Soma and Mangala revolve around
               Chandramukhi. This part will be staged in
               Opera style.]

Chandra   : Oh, side, please. I will go.

Mangala   : She is leaving.

Minister   : (To Soma) Duhshasan-Let Draupadi reach
               the Royal Court.

Soma   : Sir, your order must be obeyed.

[Soma pulls Chandramukhi's sari. Out of anger, she slaps him.]

Chandra : You...Bastard...

[Ramadas's voice is heard.]

Voice : You love me, but you can't die for me.

[Chandramukhi becomes conscious. Suddenly, she is helpless. Ravi, Soma and Mangala get hold of him. Soma is pulling her hair.]

Soma : Come with us.

Chandra : No, please leave me.

Minister : Duhshasan, 'Disrobe Draupadi in the Royal Court.'

Chandra : No...no...no

[Rabi, Soma, and Mangala start disrobing Chandramukhi.]

Minister : Come fair-complexioned Draupadi (For Chandramukhi), sit upon my right thigh.

Chandra : (Crying out for help) Ramdas...Ramdas

Rabi/Soma/Mangala : Can Ramdas save you? (Laughing)

[Stopping Chandramukhi's mouth with their hands, they take her into the bedroom. Her cry in distress is heard. The stage is empty. Actor-III comes at that time.]

Actor III : Is the Minister there?

[Petticoat and blouse fall upon him from inside.]

Is the Minister there?

[An empty wine bottle comes rolling to him.]

Oh my God! Is the Minister there?

[Minister's voice is heard inside.]

Minister   : Now you can go.

Actor III   : Oh-[Actor-III comes out of the room in shame. Rabi, Soma and Mangal come to the stage immediately. Minister's dress is unrestrained.]

Minister   : She is ruined.

Rabi   : Yes

Soma   : We have finished our work.

Mangala   : Neither will there be any bamboo, nor will the flute be played on.

[Actor-III has come.]

Actor III   : Sir-

Minister   : What happened? Who are you? Who has allowed you to come at this moment?

Actor III   : Sir, I am Ramdas.

Minister   : Which Ramdas? I don't know you.

Actor III   : Sir, I am Gandhi. You had sent me to the High Land Areas to campaign for the Election. I had worked there for twenty days.

Minister   : What are you doing there? Election Campaigning?

Actor III   : No, Sir. I was cooking for the workers.

Minister   : I don't know that. Go to them for whom you were cooking food.

Actor III   : Sir, you have sent me there. You told me to give twenty-five rupees per day.

Minister   : My candidate was defeated in the Election. Will I give you five hundred rupees? I don't know you. Go away from here.

Actor III   : Please listen to me, Sir. My wife was admitted to the hospital. For her treatment, I came to you to work. I stayed in the village for twenty days. I got the news; she is earnest. I am not requesting you for help. I have worked for you. Please pay me that amount.

Minister   : Don't irritate me. Will you go from here? Or else I will call the Watchman.

Actor III   : Be kind and compassionate to me, Sir.

Minister   : Ok. Take this ten rupee note.

Actor III   : Ten Rupees?

Minister   : Then five hundred. Where do the beggars come from?

Actor III   : Sir, I am trying to live with much difficulty
                  as a gentleman. I have given up
                  hooliganism. I am not involved in sinful
                  activities. It is tough to live such a life. Still,
                  I have faith. I am not begging you for alms.
                  Can anyone beg to wear Gandhi's dress? I
                  am asking for the value of my labour.
                  Please, let me live honestly. Please don't
                  spoil my hope.

Minister   : Oh, this man has maddened me now. Will
                  you go from here or not?

Actor III   : Is this the value of my request?

Minister   : You bloody fool.

                  [Minister throws the wine bottle to
                  Ramdas's face.]

Actor III   : (Out of anger) Sadananda Baliar Singh.
                  You are insulting Ramdas, until now. I
                  tolerated. But, now you have insulted
                  Mahatma Gandhi's dress. The attire I have
                  worn is of the 'Father of the Nation'. You
                  have poured wine on that dress.

                  [Ramdas takes off his goggles and shawl. He
                  holds the staff tightly]

Rabi/Soma/Mangala   : What are you doing?

Actor III   : I will be in the get-up for the Ramdas you
                  want.

Minister   : Ramdas-

                  [Actor-III, taking his hands up, looks around
                  helplessly.]

Actor III   : Hey, Mahatma Gandhi, please forgive me. Though I tried hard, I couldn't live. I can bear my insult, but not yours. This staff upon which you have been dependent to bring Independence to the country and to follow the path of non-violence is going to be the weapon of violence today.

Minister   : What are you doing?

[Actor-III, holding the staff, comes forward.]

Actor III   : I am not Gandhi; I am Ramdas. I am the hooligan Ramdas. I have taken off Gandhi's cover. I have come down to the road. *Jay Maa Kali!*

[When Ramdas raises the staff to beat the Minister, Chandramukhi, running from inside, stops him. Her body is blood-stained. She is unable to stand.]

Chandra   : No…Ramdas…no…

[Ramdas stops suddenly. He is surprised to see Chandramukhi here with her blood-stained body. When Chandramukhi falls on the ground, Ramdas gets hold of her.]

Actor-III   : How are you here, Chandramukhi? What has happened to you?

Chandra   : Don't ask me anything. If I open my mouth, you will again become Ramdas. One day, you were saying, 'I love you. Can I not die for that love?' Today, I am dying for that love only, Gandhi. Please don't ask me anything.

Actor III   : (Roaring) Chandramukhi- Please tell me what happened. Who is responsible for your condition?

Chandra   : I have nothing to say. I have promised I won't tell you what has happened to me. Gandhi, you asked me one day, "Can there be love without body?" My body is ruined, but love can reign.

Actor III   : Chandramukhi-

Chandra   : Gandhi, for my sake, you won't be Ramdas ever.

[Chandramukhi can't say anything. Her throat shivers. My eyes are getting closed. She gently extends her hands to touch Ramdas's feet but can't. While shedding tears, she falls. Ramdas touches her body. She is no more. He shouts out of anger and unhappiness.]

Actor III   : Chandramukhi

[While crying, he falls upon Chandramukhi's body.]

Minister   : What were you all doing? (Asking Rabi) How could Chandramukhi come here?

[Ramdas raises his face up from Chandramukhi's body.]

Rabi   : Quit the place.

Soma   : Inform the police.

Mangala   : I am going (When Mangala advances, Ramdas obstructs him with his staff.)

Actor III   : No…no…

[The Minister with Rabi, Soma, and Mangala are startled—the entire body of Ramdas trembles in anger. The stage's lights change and hints of the storm appear. Ramdas displays his apocalyptic pose of destroying the world. The rhythm of the hysterical, frantic dance is played on. Ramdas's every limb reflects that pose.]

Voice   : *"jaṭā bhujaṅga piṅgaḷa sphuritphaṇā maṇiprabhā,*

kadamba kuṅkuma dravapralipta digvadhumukhe,

madāṁdha sindhura sphuratvaguttariyamedure,

manovinodambhutam bimbhartu bhūtabhartari."

English   :"May I find incredible pleasure in Lord Shiva, who is the advocate of all life,

With his creeping snake with its reddish-brown hood and the shine of its gem on it,

Spreading variegated colours on the beautiful faces of the Goddesses of the directions,

That is covered by a shimmering shawl made from the skin of a vast, inebriated elephant."

All : Ramdas, you leave the place.

[Ramadas is looking upward in anger and obsession.]

Actor III : Gandhi, you could not save Ramdas.

Minister : (To all) What do you look at? Holding him informed the police.

Rabi : Leave the place.

Soma : We will hand over you to the police.

[Mangala rings the phone.]

Minister : Ramdas-leave the place safely. Otherwise, I will ruin you.

[Ramdas picks up the staff from the ground. He is mentally prepared to return to his earlier state of hooliganism.]

Actor III : *Ramdas Jindāvād* (Ramdas Live long)

Ramdas Jindāvād (Slightly louder)

Ramdas Jindāvād (Loudly)

Minister, you scoundrel, rascal! You will supply wine and women a thousand times to get votes from my area. How did you pour wine in my face? Now you are with pride. And you, all bastards of Bhagabanpur, have given me tips a thousand times about continuing your business. You have surrendered before me. I have urinated, you have drunk, and you are so powerful now. How dare you kill my wife? I will kill you all now and chop you into pieces. I will feed the dogs your flesh soon.

All : Please, Ramdas, pardon us! Pardon us!!

Actor III : Hand over your wives and daughters to me. Taking them, I will do my business in this city.

All : We will send them to you once we leave the place.

Actor III : You, bastards- You have sold women and girls for money. Do you think Ramdas as you are? Let your money go to hell. Sweepers also earn money for their profession. You are worse than them. I will kill you hammering one by one.

[He raises his staff. All are moving helter-skelter to save their life. At that time, a Police Inspector reaches there with a revolver.]

Inspector : Ramdas- Be aware of the law.

Actor III : They have killed my wife. I will kill them.

Inspector : The law will take its course. Shut up now.

Actor III : No-(When Ramdas tries to beat the minister with his staff, the Inspector triggers the revolver at Ramdas. The bullet hurts Ramdas's left hand. The staff falls from his hands. He calms down in pain. He glances

over Chandramukhi's face. Chandramukhi's
voice reverberates.)

Chandramukh's voice: For my sake, you will never be
Ramdas again.

[Rabi, Soma, Mangal and Minister come to
the Police Inspector for their safety. Ramdas
raises his head.]

Actor III   : All right, Inspector. They have killed my
wife. You are saying, 'The law will take its
course.' I have faith in law because the
world runs in faith. I know the culprit
always wears a garland, and the innocent
Gandhi is punished. You have brought
awareness to me. The road is so long that
there is no end to walking. Let's see whether
I can reach or not.

[Ramdas's eyes are tearful. He holds
Chandramukhi's one hand.]

Chandramukhi, you come. We have to walk
along.

[Later, he becomes conscious and sits down
at Chandramukhi's dead body.]

After that, Ramdas kisses Chandramukhi's
forehead. At that time, *Ramdhun* is heard
from a distance.

*"īśwar āllah tere nām, sabko sanmati de
bhagbān,*

*raghupati rāgham rājārām, patitapāban
sitārām."*

[Ramdas wears the goggles and shawl and stands up holding his staff.]

Get up, Chandramukhi. *Ramdhun* is heard at a distance. Perhaps the night comes to an end.

[*Ramdhun* is heard at total volume. The sun appears in crimson in the east. Ramdas is looking at the rising sun.]

END

Gandhi in Odisha

DRAMATIS PERSONAE

Mahatma Gandhi   : A Freedom Fighter

Gopabandhu Das   : A Social Activist and a Freedom
Fighter

Braja   : A Journalist/Stage Manager)

Jadu   : An ordinary man of Dabhar Village

Madhusudan Das   : A Freedom Fighter

Neelakantha Das   : A Freedom Fighter

Madan   : A wood seller of Bolagada

Gopabandhu Choudhury: A Freedom Fighter

Harekrushna Mahatab : A Freedom Fighter

Acharya Harihara   : A Freedom Fighter

School Master (Baleswar)

Medical Surgeon

Deputy Magistrate (A British)

Buto (A citizen of Germany)

Two Priests

Four British Soldiers

Mahadev Desai   : A Freedom Fighter

Satyagrahis/ Villagers

Lalagiri, Chandrasekhar Behera, Nrusingh Guru

Kasturba   : Wife of Mahatma Gandhi and a
Freedom Fighter

Ramadevi   : A Social Activist and a Freedom
Fighter

Female Barber (The wife of a barber)

SCENE-I

[It's a symbolic stage. Two steps are on the back of the stage. The back is installed with cyclorama. Clamour is heard at the beginning of the scenes. All are waiting for Mahatma Gandhi to come. Slogans are heard. Bharat Mata Ki Jay! Mahatma Gandhi Ki Jay! Hindu Muslim Ki Jay! People are also engaged in conversation during the slogans.]

Common Man I: Gandhi will come.

Common Man II: For the first time, Mahatma Gandhi will visit Odisha. We are fortunate. We will see him in our eyes.

Common Man III: People have come here from far-off places with rice and flattened rice to wait for him. He is an envoy of Gods in human form. He is coming to give us freedom. Hello Brother, 'Chant the name of Hari in happiness.'

[Everywhere is heard 'Haribol'(chanting the name Hari) and 'Hulahuli' (inarticulate sound made by women on festive and auspicious occasions)-it is heard inside 'Gandhi has come; clear the road.' There is also chanting of the name of Hari. Gandhi, Kasturba, Gopabandhu and son Deba Das have come. People shower flowers upon them and show their humble submission by prostrating on the ground. Mahatma Gandhi Ki Jay. Gandhi went to the front stage, and a wooden chair was on a cot. He sits on it. People have garlanded him and Kasturba. Gopabandhu has delivered the welcome speech.]

Gopabandhu : My dear brothers and sisters of Odisha! This is 23 March 1921. It's the *Dola Purnima*; *the Holi* celebration is everywhere. The great soul for whom you have been waiting for long earnestly is now before you. Odisha has yet to develop fully in the political sphere, but in every age, Odisha is more advanced than the other states in terms of religion. From Goutam Buddha, Kabir, Ramanujan, and Sankar to Chaitanya, the great souls born in India have left their traces on the land of Odisha. Three hundred years before, rightly on this *Dola Purnima*, Lord Chaitanya came to Odisha to propagate the 'Religion of Love' on the bank of the Kathajodi River. Today, after three hundred years, another great soul has come to proclaim and propagate the 'brotherhood in politics'. Please try to understand him. I believe, 'We will get our *Swaraj*.'

[Gandhiji delivers his speech while sitting.]

Gandhi : My friends! I am talking of that '*Swaraj*'. Until we experience freedom in social life, how can we realize 'what *Swaraj* is all about'? If the British people instruct us on what we will eat, what we will drink, what we will think, and what we will wear, we can't achieve '*Swaraj*'. For that, we need 'Non-Cooperation', and this non-cooperation movement will help us on the path of righteousness to attain '*Swaraj*'. I want self-sacrifice and self-purification. My religion is to punish that oppressor who dominates in the political sphere. The swords cannot control tyrannical rulers. They will be weak and lose power if we are distanced from them. For that, I have brought seven proposals to your notice. People should return their awards and medals to the Government. Those who are chosen send their 'Resignation Letter' to the Government. Boycott the Government festivals. You should withdraw your children's admission from government schools. The lawyers are advised to boycott the foreign courts. The members of the newly constituted council are requested to cancel their membership. Boycott the 'foreign goods'. Then, our movement to attain '*Swaraj*' will be successful.

[Let there be a victory for Mahatma Gandhi!]

Gandhi   : Nay; say, "Bharat Mata Ki Jay!" We salute Utkal Janani!!

[Slogans are heard everywhere.]

Gandhi   : Gopabandhubabu, please come; we will join the meeting arranged by Binod Bihari.

[Kasturba, Dev Das, Gopabandhu and others are in queue following Gandhi. The chanting of the name 'Rama' is heard inside.]

"vaiṣṇav jana to tene kahiye, je piḍi parāyī jāṇere"

[All have reached the backstage like a procession. The chairs are removed from the front. The people who have accompanied him are now the audience.]

Gandhi : Gopabandhubabu, please start the meeting.

[There is a big round of applause.]

Gopabandhu : You are clapping profusely here out of respect, having seen the great soul of India amongst us. But I know the British Government is afraid of the 'clapping of the Indians'. One day, thirty-three crores of Indians learn how to clap simultaneously, and the British Government will be nowhere in the country. When there was a drought in Puri, the Government was silent. But Mahatma Gandhi himself came to inspect the conditions of Odias. Let's come to hear from him.

Gandhi : I saw the drought in Odisha. While English officials stay comfortably in their apartments, ordinary people wander helter-skelter with their skeletal bodies. They live from hand to mouth. The scene hurts me a lot. I am a saint only. I am collecting money for them along the length and breadth of India. I will ask people to "Please come to Odisha and look at the conditions of Odias." The place where filigree works, weaving saris, and sculptural works are produced, the people of that art and culture\, the state of Odisha, are poor. Today, I saw that my sisters were wearing ornaments. The ornaments are not women's decorations, but when the soul gets adorned with 'Truth and Peace', what's the need for those external decorating elements? Those may be useful for the welfare of the poor/state. So, all my dear brothers and sisters, donate what you can. Kasturba, you, please move.

[Kasturba moves toward the people. Women are taking off their ornaments from their bodies. Some donate 25 paisa coins and some fifty paisa coins. She brings all those donations to Gandhi. He watches them all and says in a trembling voice.]

Gandhi : This is not coin/money; this is not the ornament. This is the blood of people with low incomes. One day, we will attain 'Swaraj' by the blood they have sacrificed.

Gopabandhu : The meeting is over. If you have any
queries, you can ask Gandhiji.

[One Journalist named Braja comes to the
front.]

Braja : I have a question for you, Gandhiji-

Gandhiji : What do you want to ask?

Braja : You are telling us to give up education.
What will we do if the 'Non-cooperation
Movement' goes in vain?

Gandhi : If this movement becomes unsuccessful,
when you quit education, you must
realize that you are far away from sin.
Staying away from the devils, you are
doing your duties.

Braja : If I quit education, the native state rulers
of Odisha will confiscate my father's
properties. Should I see my father suffer
in this type of danger?

Gandhi : When Ramachandra was in exile for
fourteen years in the deep forest, had
Dasaratha thought of what would happen
to his properties? He had gone to the
forest to establish 'Truth and
Righteousness' in society. If the King of
Gadajata anchala (the native states) of
Odisha confiscated the father's properties
for his son's attitude, your father should

126

carry on head the danger. Once the country becomes independent, the ruling authority (of the Kings) of the native states of Odisha will disappear or vanish.

Braja   : We must learn English to get a Medical Science degree. How will we be educated about the patient's health without English?

Gandhi   : You are thinking of the health of the patients. We are preparing medicines for 'Mother India's Health'. This medicine is essential for thirty-three crores of people struggling to get food.

Braja   : Gandhiji! English Education System has already affected the backbone of national life. It has brought unity among different communities. You are still saying this is bad.

Gandhi   : The objectives with which the British Government has passed the education policy are reversed. If the English had not come to our country, like other countries, we would have developed naturally in our way. We could have learned English to learn about that country's culture and literature, had the Mughals ruled the government. You read English but like an Indian nationalist. Remember your country. Don't be a slave to them.

Braja   : But are Bal Gangadhar Tilak, Ramamohan Ray, and you not the products of the English Educational System?

Gandhi   : This question erupts in the minds of many Indians like you. Had Tilak and Ramamohan not been in the English Educational System, they would have been more powerful and influential than they are today. Are Chaitanya, Adi Shankaracharya, Kabir and Nanak not contributing to English education? If Tilak and Ramamohan stand before them, they will seem to be the dwarfs.

Braja   : What do you say?

Gandhi   : This education has made us weak and powerless. The people of the country who are getting educated in English here in India can't do what Shankaracharya alone has done. Could the English Educational System make a character like Guru Govinda Singh or a community as created by Nanak?

Braja   : Why are you saying the English Educational System has made us weak and powerless?

Gandhi   : Furthermore, it has blocked our mental growth. We have been made effeminate.

During the rule of Akbar, the Great Rana Pratap was born. While Aurangzeb was ruling, Chhatrapati Shivaji was born. But during the British Rule of one hundred and fifty years, have you seen a single person like Rana Pratap or Shivaji? The Kings of the native states of Odisha salute the political agents during the British Raj.

Braja   : What will you say about yourself?

Gandhi : Forget about me. I know the loss I have suffered without learning Sanskrit and Hindustani. It is the need of the hour to stop the Educational System that makes the learners the slaves to others.

[All start saying, 'Mahatma Gandhi! Ki Jay' All are silent. Braja has come to the front to say.]

Braja   : Mahatma Gandhi first visited India on 23 March 1921. From 23 March onwards, he visited Bhadrak, Puri, Cuttack, Satyabadi and Brahmapur.

SCENE-II

[It's the Bana Bidyalaya Campus. Food is served on a banana leaf. Gopabandu is going to have food. One person who is hungry and wearing ragged and worn-out clothes reaches there. He is Jadu. Jadu knocks on the door.]

Jadu   : *dāse āpaṇe- dāse āpaṇe* (This phrase is respectfully used only for Pandit Gopabandhu Das)

Goapabandhu   : Who are you, my son?

Jadu   : I am Jadu Dabhar. I stay in this village.

Gopabandhu   : What has happened to you? Why have you come to me?

Jadu   : In our village, fifty-nine families used to live earlier. We were four hundred and eleven people altogether. There was a drought due to the shortage of rain. Eleven children died without getting any milk. Fifty-eight people passed away not getting food. The situation compels sixty-one people to leave their motherland. We are the rest to live here. Sir, some houses in our village lie vacant. Some people have not thatched their houses.

Gopabandhu   : Is this disaster in the land of Lord Jagannatha? How do you live?

Jadu   : Women have no saris to wear. They can only step out with saris. We live on grass leaves. Sir, I am starving now. I have had my food a week before.

| Gopabandhu | : Wait for a while, my son! |

[Gopabandhu donates, taking the entire banana leaf served with food for him.]

| Gopabandhu | : Please take this. |

| Jadu | : Rice (He is eating like a beast.) I got rice after several days. (Jadu leaves taking the leaf.) |

| Gopabandhu | : O my Lord Jagannatha! When will the natural calamity disappear from my land? |

[Gnadhi and Kasturba come there.]

| Gandhi | : For the hungry, Swaraj is a fistful of rice for their belly. |

[Taking a turn, Gopabandhu sees Gandhi and Kasturba before him.]

| Gandhi | : It is the duty of those who feel proud of being Indians to serve any part of India that suffers. |

| Gopabandhu | : What can be done for these people? Though the British Government knew all this, it didn't declare the region 'Drought-prone Area'- |

| Gandhi | : Then what do you think of doing for them? |

Kasturba   : Today, you may give them the food. Tomorrow, they will ask somebody else. If they don't get it, they will starve. Otherwise, they will commit crimes.

Gandhi   : We need to provide food to the person who is hungry to solve his problem. We are making him lazy in life. He will never try to get food. So help him get a job. Show him how to earn money in life. Then, he will get a way to live. And that source will be a spinning wheel.

Kasturba   : The Ryots in Champaran of Bihar were oppressed by the Indigo Cultivators. Nowadays, they earn their livelihood by spinning their wheels.

Gopabandhu   : You are right, Gandhiji. Let the 'Charkha Movement' (Spinning Wheel Movement) be started in Odisha. Our slogan will be: "Work hard to get food and stitch clothes to wear."

Gandhi   : I want to say, "Let Odisha be the storehouse of *Khadi* and food for the entire Bharatavarsa." We all will quit foreign goods. Once upon a time, this state of Odisha was the country's storehouse. Thousands of rice packets were exported outside from Balasore, Odisha. Today, in this disaster or drought, let the spinning wheel be the source of income. We will collect funds for this. We will provide people with the spinning wheel. Don't worry about selling the clothes. I am taking the onus of that.

Gopabandhu : Gandhiji, like Bhagiratha, you have helped the Ganga of Progress flow in Odisha. Your wish will be fulfilled. The 'Charkha Movement' will start in Odisha.

[All the characters on stage remain as they are. Braja comes to the front. He says, standing in a zone. There is darkness behind him.]

Braja : Keeping this view, Pandit Gopabandhu Das writes a poem:

"Stop not walking on the path of Truth and Righteousness,

All the people call for Panchayats from village to village,

Concentrate on spinning the wheel, removing fear from the mind,

Give up all kinds of disparities based on caste and contempt,

Bad habits like theft, women harassment and taking liquor,

Don't spoil and pollute the peaceful village surroundings,

The practice of this will bring happiness and glory to all,

Monsoons will come to us with a shower of rain in time."

Gandhiji's first visit ended on 30 March 1921. At the invitation of Utkal Gaurav Madhusudan Das, he came to Odisha for the second time on 19 August 1925.

SCENE-III

[Gandhiji sees Madhubabu's Utkal Tannery. Madhubabu and Mahadeva Deshai accompany him]

Gandhi : I have visited your Utkal Tannery, Mr Das. You are very courageous in setting up a handicraft industry in a poor state like Odisha. Where have you got such an idea?

Madhu : Land never increases in Odisha, but the mass population increases. The people here need help with having food. So, to address the public issues, many industries and factories should be set up. If we plough the land, we can have the agricultural products. But industrial growth will happen in the regions if we use our hands.

Gandhi : I agree with you.

Madhu   : But people must understand the differences between agriculture and industrial growth. If the youth needs to understand the importance of labour and hard work, they will be energized. That's why I support the 'Charkha Movement'. I first recruited English people in my industry. Now, seventy-five unemployed youth work here.

Gandhi   : Yes, Bengal Satish Chandra Dasgupta had worked a lot in this direction.

Madhu: Our work style is the same. Here, the shoes are made from dead cows and bull hides. We have prohibited cow slaughtering. We don't receive the hides of those cows that the Butcher slaughters.

Gandhi   : Do you do the work?

Madhu   : I have got training, and I train others.

Gandhi   : If I want to know it from you, can you train me to establish a tiny tannery at Sabarmati Ashram?

Madhu   : If you want, I will help you learn.

Mahadeva   : I am surprised that a knowledgeable person like you does not support our 'Non-cooperation Movement'. We are different from each other in opinions.

Madhu   : Because of my conscience, I can't support this movement.

Gandhi   : I know you don't hold up our Non-cooperation Movement, but I respect your thoughts and ideology as you think of Odisha's development.

Madhu   : I aim to make a perfect Odisha State. Gandhiji! You see, now there is nothing like Odisha State. Cuttack, Puri and Balasore are under the Banga Presidency. Ganjam and Koraput are under the Madras Presidency. Seven Native states, along with Sambalpur, are under Madhya Pradesh State. Where are the borders of Odisha? In which language will the children of the Tribal Communities residing within our territory get an education? Though we have raised this issue repeatedly, we are still waiting for someone to listen to us.

Gandhi   : I have only read Odisha's name in one of Rabindranath Tagore's poems. Besides this, people from other states need to learn more about Odisha. I have been raising this issue at Congress meetings. I strongly support you and extend my cooperation for the reorganization of Odisha State based on language in different meetings. That is why the Odisha Pradesh Congress Committee is constituted to get approval from the Odisha State at the National Politics.

Madhu   : I have repeatedly raised this issue before
the Bengal Presidency. But nobody pays any
heed to us.

Mahadev   : You all are responsible for that. After you
have accepted the Bihar-Odisha State
ministerial position, many people have
opposed this.

Madhu   : I don't care about others who think of me
differently. I will certainly do what is right.
My main problem is that my tannery factory
runs with a loss of Rs. 1 20,000/- .

Gandhi   : Gopabandhu Babu has also opened a
school at Satyabadi. It becomes difficult to
collect funds for that nowadays. Then I will
tell Ghanashyama Das Birla about you. If he
buys a portion of your company, your
problem will be solved.

Madhu   : Thank you, Gandhiji! Today you are
staying with my family.

Gandhi   : That has already been decided before. Let's
move.

[Gandhi smiles. Others stand still. Braja
comes to the front stage.]

Braja   : Kuntala Kumari Sabata writes in a poem
about Gandhiji's visit to Odisha:

"O Indian Soldier Narayani! You wake up; Gandhi is your leader, in the name of Vishnu;

Mohan Karam Chand Gandhi, the great saint, is your companion today in your battle of righteousness."

On 20 August, Gandhi left Odisha. For the third time, he visited Odisha on 03 December 1927. On this tour, he had planned to visit Paralakhemundi, Brahmapur, Aska, Gobara, Purushottampur, Boirani, Polasara, Kallikote, Kodala, Rambha, Bolagada, Khordha, Jatni, Puri, Balasore, Bhadrak, and Baliapal. Before coming to Bolagada, he addressed the students in a meeting at Brahmapur on 04 December.

SCENE-IV

[Gandhi sits on the stage of the Students' Union Meeting at Brahmapur. Gandhiji starts addressing the masses.]

Gandhi : Professors, Students' Union, My Brothers!!! The activities of this meeting are different from those of other meetings. We have collectively done the morning and evening prayers at the Satyagraha Ashram for the last few years. As our body needs food, so our soul needs prayer. One can live without food for some days, but one inclined to God can't live a moment without prayer. The lack of prayer absorbed in thoughts of the true soul is why today's world is full of strife and struggle. If the students wanted to establish education truly on character-building and the foundation of true heart, for its fulfilment, they would pray to the almighty every day with their open hearts. As the collective prayer is arranged here today, I request you all to do the prayer with utmost care.

[Gandhiji sits in the posture of doing the prayer. The people are everywhere. The chanting of the name Rama is heard inside-"Vaishnavi Janata teṇe kahiye"- the place is echoed with the name of Rama.]

SCENE-V

[It is Bolagada. Two British Cops are threatening the general mob.]

Police I	: The government order states that you will not attend Gandhiji's meeting. If anyone goes, he will be imprisoned. Remember this.
Police II	: None of you will arrange any meeting or attend Gandhiji's meeting.

[Then Madan comes with a bundle of firewood on his head. His body is worn out, he has ragged clothes, and his beard is unshaven.]

Police I	: Where are you going?
Madan	: For selling firewood
Police I	: After selling the firewood, you will go home, but not to any meeting anywhere. Keep this in mind and go away.

[Madan has left. The police look around and leave the place. After a while, Gandhi, Gopabandhu and Nilakantha Das reached there. Gandhi sits somewhere.]

| Gandhi | : Gopabandhu Babu! I say you a point, 'I desire to wander many places, but my body does not allow me.' Last December 05-06, I went to Brahmapur. I addressed the students there and collected some funds. On 07 December I had gone to Purushottampur, Boirani, Polasara, Kodala and Khallikote. My health condition was not good. I rested for the whole day at the Rambha Royal |

Palace. Today, I came to Bolagada from Rambha via Banapur.

Nilakantha : The main problem of Ganjam is the conflict between Andhra and Odisha for Brahmapur. Therefore, the news of your visit has yet to be published in any newspaper.

Gandhi : Still, we have to move ahead and think of Odisha's development.

Gopabandhu : We think when the plights of Odisha will end.

Gandhi : On 15 September, I wrote to Young India. Come with me to Odisha in November. You will see the *Laat Sahab*'s residences, and ten miles away from Puri, the poor people live with skinny bodies.

[Then Madan comes with a bundle of firewood. Unloading the bundle from his head, he comes to Gandhiji. He picks up a straw from the ground and puts it in his teeth. He prostrates on the ground before Gandhiji. When he was leaving, Gandhiji said.]

Gandhi : Who is he?

Gopabandhu : He is an untouchable of the Dalit Community. Having seen you, out of reverence, he prostrates on the ground with a straw in his teeth.

Gandhi

: My head goes down out of shame for this respect. Who are you, Babu? Please come here.

Madan

: I am Madan. My village is six miles away from here. I came to sell firewood to Bolagada Market. I heard, "You have come, Sir!" The British Cops denied me to meet you. Their words did not convince me. So, I came to you.

Gandhi

: Why did you put a straw in your teeth?

Madan

: I am a Dalit. How would I respect you?

Gandhi

: I am unable to carry the respect you have shown me. What do you do? How does your family run? (Gandhi embraces Madan.)

Madan

: I have uncultivated land. I cut down the trees from the forest and sell them in the market daily. We don't get rice to eat. We eat the meat of the dead cows and monitor the lizards killed in the jungle.

Gandhi

: Very disgusting! Why are you eating all these?

Madan

: What else will we eat? Our community people eat all these.

Gandhi

: Do you take liquor?

Madan   : I have heard the Gora Sahabs take liquor. Where will I get money for this? Sometimes, I take indigenous wine extracted from date palm trees.

Gandhi   : You have come here to respect me. When you respect the elders, you must pay something. Can you offer me something?

Madan   : Are you talking of 'donation'?

Nilakantha   : Gandhiji talks of offering 'dakshina' (honorarium given to elderly others).

Madan   : Yes, I will. I have earned an *aṇā* (6.25 paisa) selling the firewood.

Gandhi   : I don't need your paisa. I need something more valuable than this from you. Will you share?

Madan   : Yes, I will.

Gandhi   : From today onwards, you will never put a straw in your teeth before anyone. It disrespects one. It equals man with animal. You promise before me.

Madan   : I swear to give up.

Gandhi   : You won't eat the meat of dead animals and take the fermented juice of date palm tree.

Madan   : If I don't take the native liquor and eat meat as practised by the community people, I will be driven away from others.

Gandhi   : Let them excommunicate you.

Madan   : Where will I stay?

Gandhi   : Leave your village. Spin clothes in the spinning wheel. Promise me that you will be independent and work hard.

Madan   : Sure; I will surely do so.

[Then he gets disturbed and clasps a tree nearby.]

Madan   : O my tree brother! You are not ignoring me. You have never denied me your shade. O river! You have never denied me the right to drink water from your streams. O, Mother Earth! You have never forgotten me to rest you. But these people are like me and of the higher caste. But they are distancing me. They didn't allow me to enter their home. What does this mean? What does this mean?

[Madan is disturbed. Gandhiji sees him leaving the place.]

Gandhi   : Shame! Our shame!! Their Shame!!! The shame of this race!!!! We and the British Government are the shareholders of this.

[Then Gopabandhu Choudhury and Ramadevi reach there.]

Both of them: We say 'pranam' to Bapuji!

Gopabandhu   : What's about the meeting?

G. Choudhury : Today, Godavarish Mishra has arranged for a meeting. But the British police have threatened people everywhere that none of them will turn up at the meeting.

Nilakhantha : Not only the British Police but the kings of the native states and the Zamindars who are in liaison with them. They have been the brokers to the British Government out of fear of losing their chairs/ Power.

Rama   : I wandered door to door to help the women understand this for the last week. They wanted to meet Gandhiji. But today, out of fear for the police, they are not stepping out.

Gopabandhu : The British Government is afraid of Gandhiji. Can they think the movement will be stopped by threatening ordinary people?

G. Choudhury : We will discuss this later. Only a few people were visible at the meeting. How will the meeting be organized? Apart from that, the arrangement available at the Dak Bungalow of the District Board is yet to be confirmed.

Nilakantha : The oppression of the police is to be
stopped.

Gandhi : Why are you afraid? You have not
committed any crime. Think of "Let the
sleeping dog rest." This thought has been
derived from fear. Nobody can harm you
When you forget to be afraid of anything.
Lord Curzon once said, 'The people of the
land never voice for a movement.' But
throughout the country, agitation goes on. If
the Police come to threaten you, you can ask
what they will benefit from this. If they
rebuke you, let their scathing remarks fly
smilingly. Never surrender to them because
fear is more dangerous than disease. The
man afraid of other men is not a man at all.
Do not fear only for God. We may not hold
the meeting today. I am here up to 2.00 pm
tomorrow. What you have to say may be
discussed here.

SCENE-VI

[It is Bhadrak. Nilakantha das, Harekrushna
Mahatab and Gopabandhu Choudhury are in
discussion.]

G, Choudhury : WE couldn't hold a meeting in Bolagada.
Due to the threat of British Cops, nobody
turned up in the meeting. There was a good

gathering at Banapur, and we collected Rs 170/- (One hundred seventy) only. At night, Gandhiji stayed at Godabarish Mishra's house.

Nilakantha : The higher caste people were angry when he accompanied the Dalits to meet Gandhiji. He may be in trouble later. For that, you tell him to be alert.

G. Choudhury: He does not have fear for that. Gandhiji's visit to Bhadrak will be successful. How was your trip to Balasore, Mahatab Babu?

Mahatab : Gandhiji reached Balasore on the 14th morning. We requested he stay at Mukunda Prasad Das's house as a guest. C. F. Andrews, Horace Alexander, and Reverend Takk reached there by then. That day, he addressed the audience at the General Meeting and the meeting organized by the women. After that, he had to return to Bhadrak. Because he couldn't go because of his blood pressure, Kaka Kalekar went instead.

Nilakantha : How will you take him to Charbatia now?

Mahatab : I have made an arrangement for him to have a motorbike.

Nilakantha : It is good. Have you brought the agenda we have prepared for Gopabandhu to discuss

with Gandhi? At Charbatia, we have to
discuss that matter.

G. Choudhury : Yes, our first agenda was that in Odisha
now four Khadi Production Centres are
open: First, all the Charkha Centres of All
India Charkha Association; second, the
Khadi Centre established by Gopabandhu
Das at Satyabadi, My Cooperative Centre
and the Khadi Centre run by Govinda
Mishra at Champapur Centre, How can the
number be increased?

Nilakankha : Whatever you say, Gobinda Mishra hid
himself, not joining the Dasapala
Movement. After leaving that place, he is
doing good work and staying at Gandhiji's
Ashram for some years.

Mahatab : Nilakanta Babu, I have doubts about the
Balasore Congress issues.

Nilakhantha : Are you talking about people from the
native state of Neelagiri?

Mahatab : Yes, they are resting in areas
predominately occupied by the Mughals
who are leaving the state. Nothing has been
arranged for their rehabilitation. Some days
before, the British Cops enquired about the
Prajatantra Office in Balasore. The case is
under sub judice.

G. Choudhury : For that, we are all with you. Don't worry about the case. But the main issue for us is that the pastures at Chandipur are in the name of Government Officials during settlement. Hundreds of people also oppose that.

Mahatab : If we oppose, what will we gain? The political agents of the British Government do not interfere in it. If Gandhiji had taken this up to a higher level, they may have found a solution.

Nilakantha : The British officers have taken all the lands into their possessions, and they are our people, too. Today, our movement is in this condition only for them. The ordinary people have been raising their voices against the Kanika King for many years. But the British Government has protected the King. I have planned to discuss the same matter with Gandhiji. It will be good for us to work following his advice.

G. Choudhury : Well, why will we wait here? Let's move to Charbatia- Nilakantha, you come.

[All leave the stage. Light off]

SCENE-VII

[The people of Charbatia crowd the stage, but there is no clamour. Everybody is excited to see Gandhiji. Gandhi has come. Nilakantha, Harihara and Mahatab accompany him. Having seen him, people chant the name of Hari, and women express inarticulate sounds on festive occasions. There is commotion in the public for Gandhiji.]

Mahatab : Be calm and quiet while standing up. Gandhiji has come; he will meet you and listen to your issues. So please maintain silence.

Gandhi : I have come to meet you and collect funds from you. That amount will be spent on the development of your region. I am glad that you all have contributed happily.

Person I : Gandhiji, I have to say something.

Nilakantha : Well, you say one by one.

Person II : This year, I have lost everything in the flood.

Person III : Our crops were destroyed, and domestic animals were washed away in the flood current.

Person I : The Government has hiked the taxed amount. The people are forced to go to

Kolkata.

Gandhi : I am not the King, Emperor, or British Government. I am also a wanderer like you all. I will try my best to help you all.

Person II : You are the messenger of God. If you want, you can help us.

Gandhi : I pray to God to give me energy for your faith in me.

[Gandhiji looks at someone hurriedly. He wears white clothes. He is the village schoolmaster.]

Gandhi : Who are you? Please come forward.

Master : I am the village schoolmaster.

Gandhi : What's your salary? How many children do you have?

Master : I get ten rupees. I stay with my wife and two children.

Gandhi : How do you live with that amount? What's your food?

Master : Rice and fish curry, neither dal nor any vegetables. We seldom make curry. We don't get ghee and milk.

Gandhi : Here, people also don't get rice. Do you have any other source of income? Don't hide anything from me. Do the villagers offer you something to teach their children?

Master   : No, they don't. My father from Kolkata was sending me seven-eight rupees. He passed away two years ago.

Gandhi   : How do you maintain your family for the last two years?

Master   : I live with many hindrances. Sometimes our school secretary helps me.

Gandhi   : The Secretary of the School is the landlord- a rich man. Well, he helps you take food.

Master   : My children never take food at his home. I sometimes eat at his residence.

Gandhi   : How is your village? Who lives better than you in your village?

Master   : I am next to our village's Zamindar (Landlord). Forty out of sixty families live like me. The other twenty families are impoverished. We live in this poor condition because of the flood.

Gandhi   : I don't have the power to stop the flood. I can't make any embankments. If you have courage, you quit your village and stay safe and secure elsewhere. You shift all the sixty families with you.

Master   : What will you do there?

Gandhi   : You train people to weave clothes in the spinning wheel. Let them earn something. I

will help you get the spinning wheels. I will
also send the trainers.

Master   : But why are you saying so?

Gandhi   : Your Secretary is the landlord. He is
obedient to the British people. You have
been a slave to him with a salary of ten
rupees. The education you impart is of no
use. You are training people how to be
dependent on others. A place where people
are not independent, how can we think of
'Independence of the Country'? Thus, you
first become independent.

Master: Yes, I can- surely I can do.

[The people suddenly roar.]

Person-I   : What's about us? When will Kanika King
stop his tyranny?

All   : Down, Down, Kanika King!! Down, down,
Kanika King!!!

Harihara   : Keep quiet for a while. If you give slogans
only, there will be no solution to our
problems.

[All are silent now.]

Gandhi   : I will discuss this matter with your leader,
Chakradhar Behera. He will complain to the
court if you have any objection.

Nilakantha : Now you all return. (They have left the
              place.) Inspired by your ideology, Gandhiji,
              the famous Business Tycoon Jeevramji
              Kalyanji, has donated one lakh rupees to the
              All India Charkha Association and another
              to do *khadi* business in Odisha. Jeevram and
              his wife will build an ashram in Bhadrak.

Harihara   : With him, Ishwarlal Vyas and Purubai will
              build an ashram in Sora, giving up their
              family life.

Gandhi   : I believe that one day we will get
              'Independence'. We are close to 'Swaraj'.
              Yes, Mahatab Babu, I will reach Cuttack on
              18 this month. Though I have a 'Vow of
              Silence' on the 19th, I will meet Madhusudan
              Das. I will attend the General Body Meeting
              on the 20th of this month. The lexicographer
              Gopalchandra Praharaj has invited me. I will
              stay at his residence for a day. As per our
              planning schedule, we will visit.

              [All are silent at the back. Braja comes to
              the front zone. The back side of the stage
              darkens. He says.]

Braja   : Gopabandhu Das writes a poem on
              Gandhiji's attitude to Odisha:

              "Gandhiji, realized the distressed Odias in
              heart, said to me alone in sorrow,

Having seen this harsh reality, my mind says to give up life my hunger strike.

It is better to die a hundred times than to live with the plights they are,

But I have faith that the country's sorrow will vanish soon."

Gandhi's third visit ended on 21 December 1927. Under his leadership, the Khadi Movement in Odisha continued.

SCENE-VIII

[Acharya Harihara, Gopabandhu Choudhury and Nilakantha Das discuss inside the Satyabadi School compound.]

G. Choudhury : What decision was made regarding Odisha's border conflicts?

Nilakantha : We have discussed this with Gandhiji. He said, "He will take the responsibility for this." I hope he will raise this issue at the next Congress session/meeting.

G. Choudhury : But Gandhi observed that the 'Vow of Silence' had avoided active politics since 1927. He has declared that he will work for some days to expand *Khadi*'s business.

Nilakantha : He thinks that if the condition of ordinary
people does not improve, it will only be
possible for us to continue the movement for
a short time. People do die here without
getting food. How will they join the
movement? We are very few. The British
Government is still waiting to listen to the
issues of the ordinary people. Government
officials have appeased some flatterers for
their benefit. So, it would be better for us to
execute Gandhiji's advice and orders.

G. Choudhury: I agree with your opinion. Our objective
should be to expand the Khadi business and
collect funds. I marked your *khadi* centre
running well here.

Nilakantha : Yes, Gopabandhu himself is looking after
the *Khadi* Centre. This year, we had good
Khadi garment sales at *Ratha Yatra* (the Car
Festival).

Harihara : Except that we have no other way. This
year, a flood washed away many houses,
even the railway tracks in Balasore. The
Government was silent. At that time, we
were distributing flattened rice and regular
rice, wandering from village to village. But
who will give food to people experiencing
poverty after the flood? How will they earn
their livelihood?

G. Choudhury : Gandhiji was right. How can we think of the Country's Independence where the people are not independent?

Harihara : So, the 'Swaraj' for people experiencing poverty is food for their stomachs. Today, I remember Gandhiji's words. If a person dies without getting food in a country, that country shares the sin of committing human slaughter. The English are here, the devils. For their oppression and tyranny in governance, the Odias in Odisha are in this critical condition. They need the 'Swaraj'.

G. Choudhury : We are ready to sacrifice our lives in that 'Movement'.

Nilakantha : That's why Gandhiji always praises you and Ramadevi.

G. Choudhury : Yes, Pundit Ji, you have the time to flatter me now.

Nilakantha : I am not flattering-I am saying fact. The way both of you are managing the *Khadi* Centre, they are pleased. Apart from that, the way Ramadevi has changed women's attitudes toward educational awareness of contemporary situations and handicraft development is commendable. A few women are blessed with this skill.

[Gopabandhu comes.]

All   : We say 'pranam' to *dāse āpaṇe* (A phrase mainly used for Gopabandhu).

Gopabandhu : Let Jagannath bless you all. I will attend Lahore with Lingaraj Mishra to join Loka Sevak Mandal's annual session. I have invited you all to that.

G. Choudhury : It is heard that you may get a higher post. Your name is discussed for the Vice-President.

Gopabandhu : I am a typical worker. I don't have any desire for that post/ position.

Nilakantha   : You will raise the border-conflict issue there.

Gopabandhu : I have remembered that. Nilakantha, you would take care of Satyabadi School and Satyabadi Press. The *Samaja* should regularly be published. If you have questions, you can write letters to me.

Harihara   : Gopabandhu Babu, you will take care of your health there. You have been working for the last eight years continuously and suffering from health issues repeatedly. Out of that, you spent twenty-four months in jail. If you are in good health, you can work for the country.

Gopabandhu : My country is sick today. The people of my state don't get food to eat. They are dying of diseases. How can I take care of my health here? Don't worry about me, Harihara. I am very well. The day India gets her independence, I will be entirely well.

Harihara   : You are always like this.

Gopabandhu : Let's go now. Krupasindhu is waiting for me.

[After they leave, the stage is lit off.]

SCENE-IX

[It's the Satyabadi School Compound. Gopabandhu is sleeping on a bedstead. Nilakantha, Harihara, Krupasindhu, Gopabandhu Choudhury and Ramadevi surround him.]

Ramadevi   : Gopabandhu ji, Gopabandhu's health condition does not improve. He is sick for so many days. He has not recovered fully from illness. His health deteriorates over time. He has given up taking food. Have you consulted the Doctor?

Harihara   : We have brought medicines from the Doctors and the Physicians. But there is no improvement in his health.

G. Choudhury : He did not look after his health. He was wandering with the people day and night. He didn't maintain any schedule for taking food. He was often sick. I told him, "Please take medicines, and you will recover." He didn't listen to me.

Nilakantha   : Today, I am called the surgeon from Puri. He is about to reach. Let's watch what he recommends.

[The surgeon has come holding a bag.]

Nilakanthsa   : All right. Please do come. We are all waiting for you.

[The surgeon is doing the tests. After that, he comes.]

Surgeon   : How did it happen?

Harihara   : He moved to Lahore in April to attend Lok Sevaka Mandala's Session. He was fallen sick while returning. The Odia workers in Kolkata invited him to constitute an organization. In that health, she went to Kolkota. There, he was affected by a severe fever. When all of us requested him to come, he came here. How is he now?

Surgeon   : I am sorry that his pulse rate is slow now. There is no hope of recovery.

[Nilakantha cries out.]

Nilakantha   : Doctor!

[Doctor leaves the place quietly. Gopabandhu laments.]

Gopabandhu : Nilakantha, please help me sit here.

[Nilakantha and Harihara help him sit.]

Gopabandhu : I couldn't see India's Independence. You will take care of Satyabadi School. *Bande Utkal Janani*!

[Gopabandhu falls. All lament saying 'dāse āpaṇe'. Braja is standing in the front zone.]

Braja : It's 17 June 1928. He died at 7.25 pm on Sunday, and *Netrotsaba* Day. The Utkal's ever-burning lamp flame extinguished. The most popular 'dāse āpaṇe' (Gopabandhu) breathed his last. Mahatma Gandhi writes on his death.

[Gandhi stands on the backstage. On the dead body of Gopabandhu, his writing is read out loudly in his voice.]

Gandhi : The country has become poorer by the demise of Gopabandhu. He is not with us physically, but his soul is very much alive with us. Let the great soul regulate the life of Odisha workers. Let his death, the people's attention towards his duty of service, great effort, and sacrifice bring unity among the workers who are spread all over. I convey my heartfelt condolences to all his relatives and followers for the significant loss they have borne.

Braja   : The great soul who had taught the spirit of nationalism among the Odias, the friend of the poor, Pandit Gopabandhu Das, is no more.

[Gopabandhu's poem is heard from inside.]

"Let my body mingle with the soil of the land,

Let the people of my country walk upon my back,

Let all the potholes on the roads of the country

be filled in with my flesh and bone."

[While the song goes on, Nilakantha, Gopabandhu Choudhury, Harihara, Krupasindhu and others shoulder the bedstead where Gopabandhu's dead body is. Braja is saying from the front zone of the stage.]

Braja   : That year, Gandhiji came to Odisha for the fourth time on 21 December. While making his journey from Wardha to Kolkata, he got down at Jharsuguda Railway station, went to Sambalpur and addressed the public energetically. The people of Sambalpur were pleased. But at that time, Gopabandhu was not with Gandhiji. The year 1930 was remarkable in the history of India. The Salt Satyagraha Movement was launched all over India. Gandhiji made his journey to Dandi to disobey the rules of the British Government. His influence was in Odisha. The people joined the movement and violently protested in Inchudi of Balasore District, Odisha.

SCENE-X

[Harihara, Ramadevi, Mahatab, Goapabandhu Choudhury and many Salt Satyagrahis are united in a large field at Inchudi, Balasore. Harihara starts the speech.]

Harihara : Brothers! You all know that Odisha was once rich, wealthy and prosperous and now is poor. The reason for this is the destruction of Salt Industries during the British Rule of India. Beside our house is the sea, but we can't extract salt from it. We have to pay taxes if we prepare salt from the sea. But the salt packets prepared from Liverpool will be sold in our country, and the people of our country will purchase salt, mortgaging their utensils. We can't tolerate this injustice.

Ramadevi : Today, the Salt Satyagraha starts in Balasore, Cuttack, Puri, and Ganjama. Though the British Government tries its best to suppress the movement, Shashi Bhusan Rath's edited daily Asha in Ganjam, the weekly The Samaja in Cuttack and Mahatab's Prajatantra in Balasore have published all our news broadly and reinforced our moral courage.

Mahatab : Many Satyagrahis have joined us not only from the Coastal Belt but also from Sambalpur. We had a big industry earlier. Omer says the East India Company was earning eighteen lakh rupees per annum a hundred years before. We don't get one rupee today, though we are poor.

G. Choudhury : If we don't protest the government policy that denies salt to our rice plate, we can't have salt without paying taxes. Who else can be crueller than this British Government? The Salt Act may not work in any civilized country. People have every right to disapprove and reject rules/policies unfavourable to the public's interest.

Harihar : Today, Mahatma Gandhi declared all over the country to disobey the Salt Act for Salt Satyagraha. He has started his journey from Sabarmati Ashram to Dandi. From this Balasore of Odisha, we will begin the Salt Satyagraha.

Ramadevi   : The British Government has arrested our
                  co-workers. But there is no question of
                  being oppressed by that.

                  [Suddenly, the people protested.]

Person I   : We won't obey this Act.

Person II   : The Sea is ours, and the right to extract salt
                  from the sea is ours. Nobody can deny us
                  this.

                  [Everywhere is the slogan 'Bharat Mata Ki
                  Jay' and 'Mahatma Gandhi Ki Jay'].

Mahatab   : We will start the Civil Disobedience
Movement from here.

                  [While all are marching ahead, the British
                  Deputy Magistrate and *Sepoys* are coming
                  from the front to obstruct their movement.]

Magistrate   : I warn you all. Refrain from proceeding
                  ahead. The Act 144 is on. You will need
                  help to proceed to the sea beach.

Mahatab   : There is no question of return. We will
                  extract salt from the sea.

Magistrate   : Mahatab, you know British rule very well.
                  The government knows how to control
                  protests or riots well.

G. Choudhury : No Brit can get water here if you forcefully
                  suppress the agitation.

[One sings to tease or troll the Magistrate.]

Person I : Come, who wants to buy; hey young man, you buy,

Those who want to buy can come and buy,

From the Sea Beach and the battlefield

Have reached us with your country's salt.

Magistrate : I warn you for the second time if you disobey the Act, I will lathi-charge here to break up the protest.

Person II : "Before our iron hearts, your wooden lathi stands nowhere,

You know we have friendship with 'Death'; 'Pain' is our friend."

All : *'Bande Mataram'*

[While advancing, saying so, the English Soldiers obstruct them. They are lathicharging. They have beaten the Satyagrahis. They have pressed satyagrahis with their feet. They have caught hold of Harekrushna Mahatab and Gopabandhu Choudhury.]

Magistrate : You are under arrest, Mr Harekrushna Mahatab and Gopandhu Choudhury!

[The back zone's light is off. Braja comes to the front zone.]

Braja   : In this context, Jatiya Kabi Birakishore's poem is highlighted below:

     "See the country where Gandhiji holds a new flute

     And plays the same day and night;

     The flute calls in grief to wake up, my brother!

     Are you not any blood this day?"

The Satyagrahis of this country will never be afraid of the British Government's Oppression. The then Viceroy Irwin signed an agreement with Mohandas K. Gandhi, the leader of the Indian nationalist movement, on 05 March 1931. It is known as the Gandhi-Irwin Pact. The movement stopped. The prisoners were released. The people got back their right to extract salt from the sea, but 1935 was a memorable year in the history of Odisha. On 05 May, he went to Sambalpur from Jharsuguda. Before that, Angul Police got the news that he would go to Angul from Sambalpur. The Government planned to keep him from holding any public meetings.

SCENE-XI

[Some people are waiting to meet Gandhiji
on a road near Angul. From the front are
coming Deputy Magistrate and his team.]

Magistrate   : Where are you all going?

Person I   : Tomorrow, Gandhiji is coming. We are
going to meet him.

Magistrate   : Is Gandhiji Almighty? Is he God? Why are
you going? None of you can meet him.

Person II   : Why, sir! Many people are going. Why are
we denied to go?

Magistrate   : This is the British Government's order that
nobody can meet Gandhiji. No meeting can
be held. If you go, you will be charged a
fine; otherwise, you will go to jail.

Person I   : If the British Government is in power, why
can't it oppose Gandhiji? They will behave
like the mice before him. Why does the
Government exercise power over us?

Magistrate   : You, Rascal, are saying a lot. Return your
home.

Person II   : Empty threatening. If you arrest us, we will
                tell Gandhiji about our arrest. Let's go.

Magistrate   : What happened? Will you go? O sepoys!
                Control them.

                [Sepoys are lathicharging. They have
                returned beaten.]

Magistrate   : I have news that Gandhiji has reached
                Sambalpur. He will come to Angul
                tomorrow. No Government bungalow will
                be allotted to Gandhiji. I have told all the
                Kings and Landlords regarding this. They
                won't cooperate with him or allow any room
                for him. Pass the information to the High
                School students that the examination will be
                held even on Sunday.

Sepoy   : Sir, if they conduct any meeting under the
                tree spreading a carpet.

Magistrate   : Impossible- You roam from village to
                village and tell the people they won't come
                to Gandhiji. I won't allow Gandhiji to enter
                Angul.

Sepoy   : Yes, Sir.

Magistrate   : Come with me. We have to enquire about
                Gandhi's schedule in Sambalpur.

                [The Magistrate and the Sepoys leave the
                place.]

[A meeting stage is held at a place in
Sambalpur. Gandhi is delivering the speech.
Chandrasekhar Behera and Nrusingh Guru
are sitting beside him.]

Chandrasekhar: My dear brothers and sisters! Today, for
the second time, Gandhiji has toured
Sambalpur. Last time, he addressed our
sisters and students. This year, he will start
his *Padayatra* (Journey by foot) from
Srikshetra, Puri, for the Dalits. Because of
his call, the children of the General Category
are studying together with the children of
Dalits. A hostel has been launched at
Sgraddhakar Supakara's storehouse. We
demand the reconstitution of the state based
on language and the integration of the
Bichhinnachala (Cut-off areas). I request
Mahatmaji to start his speech.

Gandhi   : In my last visit, I told the people of
Sambalpur on the Mahanandi River bank
that if you tear Hanuman's heart, you will
see the name of Lord Rama written there.
You tear my heart; you will find *Daridra-
Narayan* there. This time, I have made my
journey to remove the evil social practice of
untouchability. The Hindus of higher caste
have developed this kind of discrimination
for the ones of lower birth. Taking liquor or
wine is also an evil practice in society.
There is nothing more terrible than the wine.

Laziness is also grouped in this category.
Laziness is the sound reason for Utkal's
poverty.

[At this time, a Brahmin comes to quarrel
and oppose. Others have driven him away.]

Gandhi   : If you understand me, we will fight against
                     untouchability. Then, people who want to
                     donate can donate what they are capable of.
                     May it be of one paisa or two paisa!

[The people leave the place after donating
something.]

Chandrasekhar: Mahatamaji, your schedule was to move
                     from Sambalpur to Angul. Your
                     accommodation was at Debendrababu's
                     house. But Angul's Deputy Commissioner
                     has instructed him to leave the room to you.
                     What shall we do now?

Nrusingh   : Our workers received the message through
                     Telegram. It will be better for you to move
                     to Puri from Sambalpur via Kharagpur than
                     via Angul.

Gandhi   : Why are you telling me so?

Chandrasekhar: You were not allowed to stay at Angul. If
                     the message gets spread outside, Odisha will
                     be condemned for this.

Gandhi: No, I will go to Puri via Angul. I will stay under a
tree if I don't have room. Don't worry about
me. The Deputy Commissioner of the
British Government wants me not to enter
Angul, but I will arrange a meeting there
only.

Nrusingh   : Mahatmaji! We have another message for
you: the *Sanatanis* (the followers of
Sanatana Dharma) will quarrel and make it
an issue. On the walls at Puri are 'Gandhi is
the enemy of Hindu Religion' and 'Gandhi,
You return!' Two to three people are ringing
the gongs for the public to understand that
they should not go to attend your meeting.

Chandrasekhar: Many social workers are moving from
Cuttack to Puri to maintain law and order.
Moreover, as there is the possibility of
showing black flags against you, many
police officers are deployed there to take
care of the situation for your safety and
security.

Gandhi   : As the *padayatra* procession for the Dalits
is a pilgrimage, what's the need for the
police to watch me? Nobody from Cuttack
should go. Only Gopabandhu Choudhury,
Mahatabji, Ramadevi and Lingarajababu
will go. I will walk on foot to my residence
from Puri Railway Station.

[Everybody is silent behind. Braja comes to the front stage.]

Braja   : For Sambalpur's brave heroes, the poet Sekhar Chintamani Mohanty writes:

The jewels of Hirakhanda State, Swaminarayan

and Abar Chandrasekhar, for me,

Have surrendered their wealth, minds and precious time,

are my good sons.

From 09 May to 08 June, Mahatma Gandhi led and continued the vast *Harijana Padayatra*. Its auspicious start was from Srikshetra, Puri.

SCENE-XII

[The stage light is on. Some people enter the stage saying 'Mahatma Gandhi Ki Jay'. Braja, coming from the front, says.]

Braja   : Don't rush. Keep quiet. Under the leadership of Gandhiji, the Harijana Padayatra will be started at 5.00 am in Puri.

It will be continued from Puri to Cuttack via Harekrushnapur, Chandanpur, Kadua, Veer Purushottampur, Dandamukundapur, Sakhigopal, Pipili, Siula, Balakati, Satyabhamapur, Balianta, Telengapentha, Kajipatana, and Gopalpur. Gandhiji will meet people everywhere. Thus, you all maintain silence and be in a queue.

[The people are standing in a queue. Then a German comes. His name is Butto.]

Braja   : Hello Brother! Who are you? Why are you here?

Butto   : I am Butto, a Naziest. I have come here from Germany.

Braja   : Why are you wandering here, not going to Germany?

Butto   : I have not gone to Germany. I met with Gandhiji at Warddha Women's Ashram; I came with him.

Braja   : What will you do here?

Butto   : I heard Gandhiji returned from South Africa. Along with some Indians, he faced General Scotts there with the weapon of 'Ahimsa'. I want to know, "What is that Ahimsa?"What does it look like?

Braja

: While wandering with Gandhiji, what did you see?

Butto

: The people surround him. They are shouting. Will Gandhiji get 'Independence' for these people? Impossible!

Braja

: Why are you saying so?

Butto

: They need to be made aware of what discipline is. Everyone in Germany is a disciplined citizen. The British Government controls the crores of Indians for this indiscipline in life.

Braja

: Then you have understood the weapon of 'Ahimsa' (Non-violence) that Gandhiji holds in life.

Butto

: No, I haven't.

Braja

: Well, you stand in that queue. You will understand everything after walking some distance.

Butto

: OK, OK, Thank you.

[Butto stands in the queue. Gandhiji has come. Nilakantha, Krupasindhu, Gopabandhu Choudhury, Harihara, Ramadevi and Mahatab accompany him.]

Gandhi

: From the 9th morning, I am starting *padayatra* for the upliftment of Harijan in Puri. Srikshetra, Puridham, is one of India's four famous and principal holy places and temples. It's my great pleasure that I am initiating my holy journey for the virtuous people from this holy Puridham. Utkal is my favourite place. I am happy about my journey here in Utkal. I have a strong feeling in my heart that the Utkal is the home state of poverty-stricken people. If I can contribute something, the lion's share of my donation will be for this Utkal. The result of my pilgrimage is immaterial to me. Still, I am confident and determined that my scheduled *padayatra* movement to uplift the Harijans/Dalits from Puri will be my best work. I am thrilled to start from Puridham. I am saying all my Sanatani Brothers all over India, the places where the Hindus question or oppose, I will never enter the temples there with or without the Harijans.

Nilakantha : Our journey starts with Gandhiji now. Please maintain discipline and make our trip a grand success. '*Bande Mataram!*'

[Everywhere '*Bande Mataram*' slogan gets echoed. It overlaps with the '*Bande Mataram*' song. All are in circles on stage under the leadership of Gandhiji. All of them halt at a place suddenly.]

Nilakantha : On the seventh day of our journey, we reached Balianta's Kunjabihari Temple.

Mahatma Gandhi will enter the temple with Harijans.

[Then two priests come.]

Priest I   : We invite Mahatma Gandhi to enter the temple.

Priest II   : This temple will open for the Harijans starting today.

[Everywhere the slogan '*Bande Mataram*' is heard.]

Gandhi   : Gopandhu Babu, I will learn Odia. Otherwise, while marching in Odisha, I need to know something.

G. Choudhury : I am giving responsibility to Godavari Devi. She will help you learn the Odia language. Please come; the temple will be inaugurated.

[Gandhi has entered. All others have entered along with him. '*Bande Mataram*' song overlaps. Then, all resumed the *padayatra*. Then, the journey halts at a point. Mahatab says.]

Mahatab   : We have now reached KajiPatana from Telengapentha. Here we have some activities. A good number of gentlewomen have come from Cuttack. They will donate their ornaments to Gandhiji's fund.

[Acharya Harihara says.]

Harihara   : Mahatmaji, a saint Lalnath from Kashmir, has come here. He wants to meet you.

Gandhi   : Please call him.

[Harihara goes to call him.]

Gandhi   : I have known Lalnath. His Guru Kalabhairav opposes me. He has passed a religious injunction for burning my photo and effigy. Lalnath opposed me while making my journey for Ajmer. The agitated mob assaulted him. I have done their treatment.

[Harihara comes with Lalnath.]

Gandhi   : Pundit Lalnathji- Have you come to show me the black flag? How many people have you brought with you?

Lalnath   : Seven or eight. Please help me.

Gandhi   : You won't get a chance here. I will give you a chance at the Kathajodi meeting in Cuttack. If needed, for your safety, I will send you some social workers. You will get permission to speak at the Cuttack Meeting. Now you can leave-

[Lalnath leaves.]

Gandhi   : Now, let's move towards Cuttack.

[Again, '*Bande Mataram*' is heard. The
padayatra ends at the meeting to be held at
the Kathajodi River bank.]

Ramadevi   : Mahatmaji's meeting will be arranged here
at this river bank. Please be seated.

[All have occupied their positions. Gandhi
sits on a wooden chair. Lalnath comes with
a black flag.]

Gandhi   : Pundit Lalnath and his friends from
Kashmir have come to Cuttack. They will
show black flags. Please don't blame them.
Allow them to sit wherever they want.

[Lalnath comes near the stage, showing the
black flag to Gandhiji.]

Gandhiji   : He is that Pundit Lalnath. Let him say first.
Then I will say. This is what our culture or
civilization is all about. That means we can
learn about religion.

[Perspiring Lalnath starts saying.]

Lalnath   : I strongly oppose Gandhiji's entry to the
temple. For that, the public treated me as a
goon or hooligan. I have come here to place
my arguments based on the scriptural texts.

Gandhi   : I am very sorry for those who say Lalnath
'a hooligan' as they are making a mistake.
All think that I have hurt the Sanatanis,

troubling their minds. I have not opposed them discussing any scriptural text. If they influence me by their arguments, I will accept their words.

[All other characters are silent. Braja comes to the front stage.]

Braja   : Gandhiji went to Patna to join the Congress Session (Meeting) in the middle of their *Padayatra*. So the *padayatra* ended there. The next journey started from Bairi Station to Bhadrak. The British Cops had tried their best to obstruct this journey.

SCENE-XIII

[It is a place in Bahukuda. A carpet is spread in a place. Gandhiji sits on it. Nilakanth, Harihara and Gopabandhu Choudhury come with him. All are seated at a distance from him. Harekrushna Mahatab comes with chapatti, milk and mango in his hands.]

Mahatab   : Bapuji, we have collected chapatti and goat milk for your food. But I only got fruits except for mango. Again, these are all sour.

Gandhi   : OK, give me the mango. (He eats the mango indifferently.)

Nilakantha Babu, if the sour taste is removed from the mango, many people would benefit from it.

Nilakantha : The renowned scientist Satish Dasgupta, who has come with us, can do this work well.

[Gandhi smiles. Then the wife of a barber comes with a razor bag.]

Gandhi : Mahatab Babu, I am waiting for a barber. Who is she?

Mahatab : Police have threatened everybody. No male persons are here. She has come to shave your beard.

[Gandhi looks at her.]

Gandhi : Well, it's ok. Can you shave my beard?

[While sharpening the razor, the woman says.]

Woman : Yes, I can. I can shave your beard the way you want.

Gandhi : OK, shave everything except the moustache.

[The woman starts shaving. Gandhiji's eyes were upon the garments she wore.]

Gandhi

: What are all these? You have worn silver bangles in your hands and gold rings in your ears. These ornaments don't suit you. The dirt from the body gets deposited on those ornaments.

Woman

: These are not mine. Today, this is an auspicious day. So I have borrowed all these. How would I come to you without wearing good ornaments? You are the King of this area.

Gandhi

: As the King, I have worn only two *khadi* garments. You won't wear these ornaments anymore. Return all these to her from whom you have borrowed.

Woman

: Ok

[Gandhi gives her 25 paisa/one-fourth of a rupee]

Woman

: Who else is here to shave?

[Mahatab comes. The woman shaves him.]

Gandhi

: What's your name?

Woman

: My name is Hema.

Gandhi

: What's your husband's name?

Woman

: The name of the elder brother of one who sits in the Jagannath Temple, Puri.

Gandhi : What does she say?

Mahatab : Her husband's name is Balabhadra. She says Jagannatha's elder brother's name.

She will not take the name of her husband.

Gandhi : Many people with good hearts stay in the unhealthy environment of the Harijan slum. Who knows them? Which saint? Nobody tries to understand them. Well, my daughter! What have you had as your food?

Woman : I have taken rice with salt. (Saying to Mahatab) your shaving is over.

[Mahatab giver her 25 paisa. She comes to Gandhi with what she has received from Gandhi and Mahatab. She sits before him, kneeling.]

Woman : Mahatma Gandhi, many people give you many things. I am a poor fellow. I don't have anything to provide you with. Please take this much I am giving you.

Gandhi : How do you give me your entire day's earnings?

Woman : You have shouldered the responsibility of the whole country if we don't give; how will you work?

[Gandhiji's eyes are full of tears.]

Gandhi

: O my daughter! What you have given is not your earnings but the blood of people like you. One day, India will gain independence from this blood. We will certainly get 'Swaraj'.

[The woman stands up.]

Woman

: '*Mahatma Gandhi Ki Jay*'

[With this slogan, she leaves the place. All are looking at her. There is darkness behind. Braja comes to the front stage.]

Braja

: The poet Mayadhar Mansingh writes a poem about the feelings of the woman barber who has shaved Gandhi's beard:

"Woman barber sees how God comes to her,
  Then, she donates her earnings to him.
  Those surrounding Gandhi start suddenly,
Surrendering their earnings at Mahatma Gandhi's feet,
  She lives the virtuous life with the blessings."

The 'Harijan Padayatra' ended on 08 June 1934. Independent Odisha State was constituted on 01 April 1936. By then, neither Utkalmani Gopabandhu Das nor Utkal Gaurav Madhusudan Das was alive. The dream/hope of the Odia people was fulfilled. Krushnachandra Gajapati was the first Prime Minister of Odisha. After two and a half months, Bishwanath Das became Odisha's prime minister. Conversely, the 'Quit India Movement' was at its peak. Gandhi came to Odisha for the seventh time to attend the Annual Day Function of the 'Gandhi Seva Sangh' at Berboi, Delanga.

SCENE-XIV

[Khadi Sammilani is over. Gandhi takes a rest at a home in Delanga. Nilakantha, Mahatab, Gopabandhu Choudhury and Ramadevi are with him.]

Gandhi : The Conference on Agriculture and Handicraft you arranged was good, Gopababu. For that, I repeatedly come to Odisha. I love the Land of Odisha. Outside Odisha, I tell others, see how human souls are reproduced and become lively in lifeless metals and horn handicrafts. The potter makes beautiful artistic handicrafts in clay. The artists and sculptors who have come to the poverty-stricken land can produce nicely designed works in bone and horns of animals and silver.

Nilakantha : Your love for Odisha could make Odisha an Independent State.

Rama   : We have faith in you and that you will bring 'Independence' to India one day.

Gandhi   : Mahatab Babu, this girl always wins my heart. She has worked so nicely in the last Harijan Padayatra that I have once expressed, 'I am in love with her.'

G. Gopabandhu   : The Odia people love you very much. Otherwise, a vast Conference would not have been possible.

Gandhi   : For that, I would like to thank you all. Now, you form the Government with your people. How is your work going on?

Mahatab   : The British Government sends a conflict between the elected Government and the Governors concerning decision-making.

Gandhi   : Once we get 'Swaraj', we will solve all our issues. Then I was happy. Chief Minister Biswanath Das said they would not depend on other states to eradicate poverty. We have already discovered our energy. Odisha stands first in Apiculture in India. Entire Odisha will be spread with beehives.

[Kasturba reached there.]

Gandhi	: Where were you so long?

Kasturba : Wife of Mahadev Desai, Durgaben, and I went to Jagannath Temple for a visit.

Gandhi : (All) Please go outside. You will send Mahadev Desai.

[Except Kasturba, all others leave the room.]

Gandhi : Did you take my consent?

Kasturba : Was there any need for your permission to visit Jagannath Temple?

Gandhi : Then clear me on what topic you will take my permission and on what you won't take.

Kasturba : I can't understand the reason for your irritation.

Gandhi : I am Hindu. I am not attending that temple because I was born in a Gujarati goldsmith caste. The reason for this is not that they denied me, but the Harijans are prohibited from entering that temple.

[Mahadev Desai comes there.]

Gandhi

: As Harijans won't enter Jagannath temple, you should not have entered that temple. He is the son of the world. Those who take food for his blessings are all his sons.

Kasturba

: I don't know that Harijans don't go to that temple. I have made a mistake entering there. I beg your pardon for that.

Gandhi

: You must have remembered- while returning from South Africa, though I had the train ticket, I was ordered to get down, say me the Black People. This racism and untouchability have been spread in the world as a disease. Sanatanis believe that untouchability is a part of Hinduism. Similarly, the Muslims and the Christians believe that except untouchability, there is nothing else in Hinduism. If you don't remove this evil practice from society, you can't solve the cases of Hindu-Muslim issues.

Mahadev

: I am sorry for Durgaben to enter the temple, Bapuji.

Gandhi

: I won't blame Kasturba. I can't pay proper attention to her education. I am responsible for her mistake. But,

Mahadev, you are writing essays against untouchability in the magazine 'Harijan'. You couldn't give Durgaben a proper education. For this reason, Maulana Saheb will say, 'Though Gandhiji tried hard to abolish untouchability from Hinduism, he could not do so.'

Mahadev : I realize her educational practice is wrong.

Gandhi : Mahadev, you know some Sanatani Pundits in Puri wrote against me on the building walls, 'I am the enemy of Hinduism.' Gandhi, you can return now. But I know that the swords oscillate over Sanatana Dharma. I am engaged in this *padayatra* in old age; its reason is not to destroy Hinduism. Its reason is to protect Hinduism. There is a danger to our religion-a sword hung over its neck. I can't sit silently at this critical moment.

[All other characters on the stage are silent. Braja has come to the front. Standing on a zone, he says.]

Braja : I remember Godabarish Mohapatra's poem here:

"Sitting on the worn-out door of fort-boundary of the inaccessible mountain,

A conjurer calls, by his sorcery, the dead to be alert from their slumber

Splitting apart the earth, the inmates of the graveyard wake up soon,

The brave souls of Khordha! You get up and raise high your heads;

O skeletons! You wake up and rise, giving up your weakness today,

Let the past glory that was stolen or no more perceptible now be revived."

Sitting inside the fort of the inaccessible mountain, conjurer Mahatma Gandhi calls 'Independence'. In his call, the entire country burns in the fire of revolution. Throughout India, the 'Quit India Movement' was. Odisha is also set on fire. While travelling from Calcutta to Madras, Mahatma Gandhi, the helmsman of this movement, got down to Odisha for the last time on 19 January 1946. He delivered his last speech for Odisha in Berhampur (Brahmapur) after receiving a broad welcome from Balasore, Bhadrak, and Cuttack Railway Stations.

[Gandhi steps up to the stage from one side on the back step. The people surround him saying 'Mahatma Gandhi Ki Jay', like a meeting. Gandhi says in the middle of the stage.]

Gandhi : I came to you all in the early morning hoping that to eradicate untouchability and spread the *Khadi* industry Odi, she will be a model for the other states to follow. I know The British Government will quit India tomorrow. If we cannot remove them from this country by our energy, what's the value of the energy we are with? That is wrong if you think of driving the English away from the government only through your voice. We can get our 'Swaraj' through the 'Truth and Non-violence' path- say '*Bande*'.

All : '*Bande Mataram*'

[Everywhere the slogan is echoed. After that, '*Bande Mataram*' overlaps. An artist fixes a national flag in the middle of the stage. On the cyclorama is written '15 August 1947.' All the artists salute the tricolour while the '*Bande Mataram*' song is on.]

END

About the Authors

Shankar Prasad Tripathy is an acclaimed and active playwright, novelist, and cultural icon of Odia Language for the last three decades. He has received the Odisha Sahitya Akademi Award for his play *Suniba Heu A Kahani*. His notable plays are *Ahe Nilasaila, Dasaabatara, Gandhinka Odisha, Ravanchhaya, Apekshare Ramachandranka,* and *Sunyapurusha.* His novel *Nadabindu* is converted into the movie *"Puskaraa".* The movie has received good response from the public recently. His Odia play *Nabakalebara* is translated into English by Black Eagle Books, USA in 2023.

Sanjeet Kumar Das: Born in Kendrapada district of Odisha, Sanjeet Kumar Das is a poet, a translator, and an educationist. His poetry collection *Asima Jeevan* was published in 2021. His translation works include Dr. Narayan Sahoo's *And the Wretched* (2023) and *Bewildered God* (2023), Dr. Niladri Bhusan Harichandan's *Salabega* and *Columbus* (2023), Shankar Tripathy's *Nabakalebar* (2024), Shankar Prsad Tripathy's *Waiting for Ramachandra* and *Sunya Purush*, Dr. Bijoy Kumar Satapathy's *Soul of Kansa* and *Kokua* (2023) Dr. Bijay Mishra's play *Niranjana* (2023) and Dr. Ratnakar Chaini's play *That Chanakya Lives (2023)*, Harihar Mishra's *Demeaned Gajapati* (2024) and Kunja Ray's *Invincible Kharavela* (2024). He has published one edited book *A Translingual Voyage: Select Indian Writings in English Translation*. Currently he works as an Assistant Professor at Department of English Language and Literature, Central University of Odisha, Koraput.

www.ingramcontent.com/pod-product-compliance
Lightning Source LLC
Chambersburg PA
CBHW031040160726
47991CB00005B/1974